THE COMPLETE PETITE

THE COMPLETE PETITE

EVERYTHING YOU NEED TO KNOW ABOUT FASHION
IF YOU'RE 5' 4" OR UNDER

JANET ATTWOOD AND MARY DUFFY

ILLUSTRATIONS BY NANCY STONE

McGraw-Hill Publishing Company

New York   St. Louis   San Francisco   Bogotá   Hamburg   Madrid
Mexico   Milan   Montreal   Paris   São Paulo   Tokyo   Toronto

1 2 3 4 5 6 7 8 9 DOH DOH 9 5 4 3 2 1 0

ISBN 0-07-002419-7

Library of Congress Cataloging-in-Publication Data

Attwood, Janet
  The complete petite.

  1. Fashion 2. Stature, Short. I. Duffy, Mary
II. Title.
TT560.A88 1990   646′.34   89-12872
ISBN 0–07–002419–7

Book design by M 'N O Production Services, Inc.

To my family,
William, Simone, Peter, and Susan Attwood,
who taught me to love words.

To my husband, Bill,
and my wicked stepchildren, Linette, Will
and Jonathon,
for their love and support.

NOTE

Although this book was written by both Jan and Mary, it is in Jan's "voice."

ACKNOWLEDGMENTS

To Faith Hornby Hamlin, our literary agent, and to Elisabeth Jakab, our editor, without whom this book would not have been realized.

Special thanks to Rita Milo, Carole Jackson, Nick Xenos, Chris D'Errico, Susan Vogel, Brigitte Grosjean, Amy Gery, Susan Brown, Deborah J. Steele, and Paris Chanelle for their invaluable contributions.

CONTENTS

INTRODUCTION

JAN ATTWOOD'S STORY—
SHORT BUT SWEET

"For what is little and well said stays fixed within the heart."
—ANONYMOUS

"No man is so tall that he need never stretch and none so small
that he need never stoop."

—DANISH PROVERB

Years ago, a well-known ballerina told me that she had been very happy to be **petite**
while growing up in wartime England. She said that her ration coupons for fabric went
further on her than on a bigger woman. She had also learned to shop for bargains in
children's shops, a habit which began to bother her only after her thirtieth birthday.

Petites are not always the stereotyped, child-sized women. They are adult fashion
customers of unique proportions with special problems and needs. In the past seven

1

years, the American clothing industry has responded to these needs with incredible speed, and the **petite fashion industry** has blossomed into the most lucrative, special-size market in the retailing world.

I was fortunate to be "in" on the beginning of the industry and to have been instrumental in many of the developments and changes in the petite market . . . and to think—I once thought being short was a disadvantage!

I remember the day when I first realized that I was short. I was an eight-year-old, a third grader, and the teacher put a math problem on the blackboard and told me to come up and solve it. I couldn't reach the problem! As I jumped up and down with the chalk, trying to write the numbers, the entire class laughed uproariously. I was immediately nicknamed "Shrimp." That nickname stuck to me for my remaining school years, along with "Half-Pint," "Peanut," "Pee-Wee," and other "shorty" nicknames. However, I optimistically thought that I would grow taller.

I attended a very strict girls' school, where we had four dances a year for which our dates were assigned to us by height. We had to descend a long staircase and our dates were presented to us at the bottom. At my last dance in senior year, my name was called, I came down the stairs, and a young man of about 6′3″ appeared. I couldn't believe my eyes! He took my arm and led me into the dance, when I was suddenly called back by the teacher. I had to go back upstairs and descend again, to be met by a fellow who had the same name but was only 5′3″ tall, which was **my** exact height. It began to sink in that I was never going to be tall, and that "short" was a detriment.

However, there are a few "perks" to being short: I can sleep very comfortably on a love seat; I can stretch out full length in the bath; I'm always in the front row in a group picture; and (perhaps best of all) I've never had to stoop or wear low heels because I wanted to make a date feel taller. I also relate well to children since I am at their eye level!

Of course, there are disadvantages, too: I'll never play the net well in tennis because the balls go way over my head; if I'm on the subway, I have a hard time reaching the rail; and my feet don't touch the floor when I sit in a chair.

I started modeling at the age of two when height was no problem. At thirteen I questioned whether I was going to grow taller, but then began commercial print work where height didn't seem to make a lot of difference: you sat in a chair or stood on a box, and most shots were from the waist up. Height didn't matter to my commercial career, but I always loved clothes and regretted not being able to be a fashion model.

Many years later I saw a Big Beauties/Little Women ad in a New York City newspaper, asking for petite women interested in modeling fashion. At that time, the word *petite* connoted a back section in a store that had a few fussy dresses and even fewer customers. Big Beauties/Little Women specified 5′4″ or under as the height requirement, so I went, was interviewed and accepted, and we began—no pun intended—in a very small way!

My first job was for a major department store, where there was no real Petite Department at all! We were dressed in small regular sizes, loaded with hats, gloves, and accessories, and were made to hold signs that said, "I'm a petite!" It was a primitive attempt to attract new customers!

My second job was at the F.I.T. (Fashion Institute of Technology) fashion show. Standing in line, about to go on stage, between two tall, willowy women, one of them turned to me and said, "What are you doing here?" I responded, "I'm a petite." She said in turn, "You're a what?" Thankfully, the music started and the show began. I was able to show everyone that a petite model on a runway looked just as good as the 5'9"–5'10" models.

Any clothing made for petites at first were prissy and unfashionable. My first fitting account put me in a size 6 regular, took my measurements, and promptly shortened the sleeves and the hem. I then came back the next week to refit the clothes, but they didn't look right. At that point, the tailors realized that a petite was not only short—her body measurements and proportions were entirely different, and they had to make new patterns.

To date, I have worked for hundreds of clients developing dresses, suits, sportswear, coats, and lingerie. Petites want to make the same fashion statements as average women, including former no-no's such as shoulder pads, cuffed pants, and pleated skirts! Everything is re-sized, from yoke placements to cuff and collar heights, buttons, and belt loops.

Most women movie stars of the Twenties, Thirties, and Forties were petite. Joan Crawford, Jane Powell, Alice Faye, Vivien Leigh, and many others had their garments tailored to their measurements, and this is what petite clothing does today. However, I have met many 5'5" and 5'6" women in the Petite Department, because petite clothes solve many of their body type problems, too. More about that later.

In this book we are going to meet some of the people who made a difference in the petite industry, including petite women who demanded clothes to fit them. These women have been a real inspiration to me. It is to them that this book is gratefully dedicated.

1

BEING PETITE

"One more short joke, and I'm going to let out one very tall yell."
—BANKING EXECUTIVE
SAN ANTONIO, 1988

That woman's sense of indignation typifies the frustration that millions of short men and women feel regarding the importance that so many people assign to height. Once considered "cute on women, but disastrous on men," shortness has found more equality among the sexes as women, struggling to emerge in the workplace, have sought the bolster of stature. Further adding to the problem of short women has been the scarcity of grown-up-lady clothes: clothes that are stylish, enduring, and chic; clothes that are designed neither for anorexic Amazons, nor for "cute, precious 'n darlin' little girls"; clothes that are **long on fashion and short on alterability**.

After more than eight years in the fashion industry, I have learned a great deal about women and fashion. More than anything, I have learned that it is not what you've got, nor how much, but what you do with it that counts.

5

But, how do you learn what to do with it?

Developing a **sense of personal style** is the best way to find the look that's right for you.

Personal style sounds easy, but few women seem to have it. We all receive mixed messages causing many of us to vacillate on the importance of appearance. For example:

- Be natural—Be glamorous
- Be yourself—Be gorgeous
- Have character—Have a face lift
- Grow old gracefully—Fight it like mad
- Develop your mind—Develop your bust

The ambivalence is unnecessary, the answer is clear. Degrees of artifice vary from woman to woman, but each woman owes it to herself to make the best physical impression that she can. First impressions are so important, and other people make judgments about us based on our external presentation.

Having personal style means that you have learned to project your *uniqueness* to others. Learning to find your personal best can be fun, educational, and even revealing.

Let's begin by exploring the most important aspect of personal style—
yourself.

2
SELF-DISCOVERY

WHAT KIND OF PETITE ARE YOU?

Statistically speaking, the average woman in the United States is 32 years old, 5'3.8" tall, 143 pounds, and size 12 to 14.

    52.5% of American women are 5'4" or less. Half of these 5'4" or less women wear a size 14 or larger, and half wear a size 12 or smaller. Each one of these groups represents a significant 26%! I call the smaller group petites, and the larger sized group women's petites (Figure 2-1).

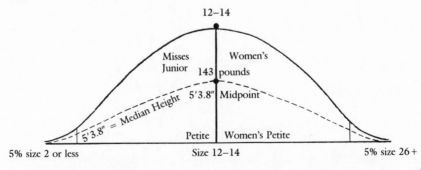

Figure 2-1 *Looking at the bell curve of sizes, one might wonder just who wears misses and junior?*

The following exercises will enable you to find out what kind of petite you are. Armed with that knowledge, you'll be able to put your best self forward. We'll explore the elements of style, grooming, fashion terms, and shopping, but first let's start with self-exploration, beginning with your body measurements.

HOW TO MEASURE YOURSELF LIKE A PROFESSIONAL DRESSMAKER

Take your measurements with a tape measure that's loose enough to move slightly (Figure 2-2). When measuring your bust, measure above the breasts under the armpits (Bust 1) and across the apex (nipples) (Bust 2). The difference between the two numbers determines your cup size in a bra. The high bust (Bust 1), not the cross-apex measurement (Bust 2), is the number of your bra (to the nearest even number).

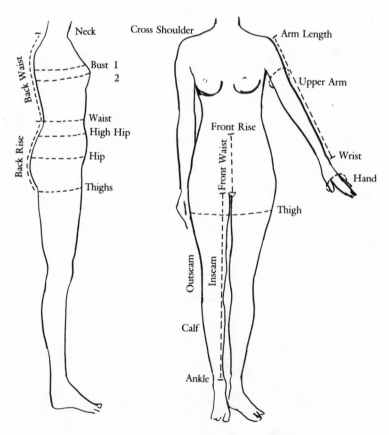

Figure 2-2 Front and back views show where measurements should be taken.

For example:

Bust 1: 32″ (going under the armpits)	Cup Chart	
Bust 2: 35″ (going across the apex)	**Difference**	**Cup**
Difference: 3″		
Bra Size: 32 or 34B	1″	AA
	2″	A
	3″	B
	4″	C
	5″	D (etc.)

When measuring your thighs, take two measurements, the circumference of both thighs together (Thigh 1) and the circumference of one thigh (Thigh 2).

The cross shoulder measurement refers to the width from shoulder tip (the bone that sticks out) to shoulder tip. Front rise refers to the center-crotch to front waist measurement, and back rise refers to the center-crotch to back waist measurement. Both of these measurements are crucial in fitting pants as front and back rises vary from person to person. The measurement around your hand at its widest part equals your glove size.

Fill out the following chart and make a copy for your wallet to refer to when shopping. It will make shopping a snap. And make a few copies for loved ones. It will give them an advantage when gift shopping for you!

YOUR PERSONAL MEASUREMENTS

Neck	_____	Thigh 1	_____
Bust 1	_____	Thigh 2	_____
Bust 2	_____	Inseam	_____
Waist	_____	Outseam	_____
High Hip	_____	Front Rise	_____
Hip	_____	Back Rise	_____
Back Waist	_____	Arm Length	_____
Hand	_____	Upper Arm	_____
Cross Shoulder	_____		

For a better look at your physical profile, try this trick used by image consultants (Figure 2-3):

TRACING YOUR FIGURE

Get a large piece of brown wrapping paper, or tape or staple newspapers together and tape the paper against the wall. Have a friend trace two outlines of you on the two

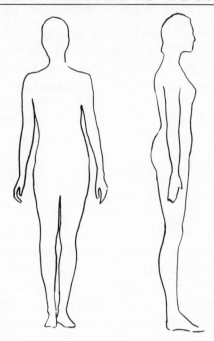

***Figure** 2-3 A trace of yourself on paper can be revealing.*

sides of the paper, one with your back against the wall, and one from profile. Use a heavy marker, so that your tracing will be easy to analyze, and be sure to wear a leotard or undies so that you get a tracing of you, not of your clothes.

When you remove the paper, take a good objective look. The woman in Figure 2-3 is short-waisted, flat-chested, narrow-shouldered, low slung in the derriere, and thigh-heavy. She looks quite average! Analyze your own tracings honestly, and you'll learn how to best suit your individual body.

WHAT DO YOU SEE IN YOUR TRACINGS?

Shoulders	narrow _____	broad _____	average _____		
Neck	thick _____	slim _____	average _____		
Bust	high _____	low _____	small _____	big _____	average _____
Midriff	flat _____	rounded _____	full _____	average _____	
Waist	small _____	wide _____	straight _____	average _____	
Hips	square _____	rounded _____	big _____	small _____	average _____
Tummy	flat _____	rounded _____	full _____		
Thighs	narrow _____	heavy _____	average _____		
Arms	long _____	short _____	thin _____	heavy _____	average _____
Legs	slim _____	heavy _____	average _____	long _____	short _____
Derriere	flat _____	full _____	average _____		

A more advanced analysis from your front tracing is worthwhile as it enables you to take a totally objective look at your proportions.

Cut your tracing so that there is no extra paper above the top of your head or below the bottom of your foot. Fold the tracing in half three times so that you have eight sections. The seven folds should hit the following places on your body for you to have what image consultants call perfect proportions. (It is helpful to know exactly where your proportions are short or long.)

Perfectly proportioned women will have the seven folds hitting at (Figure 2-4):

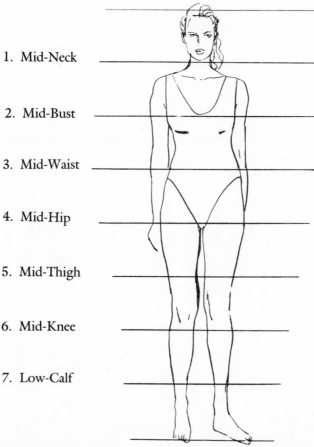

1. Mid-Neck

2. Mid-Bust

3. Mid-Waist

4. Mid-Hip

5. Mid-Thigh

6. Mid-Knee

7. Low-Calf

Figure 2-4 The "ideally" perfect proportions. Since one particularly short or long eighth can throw off your other "folds," you can also look at each section separately. Divide your total inches by 8 and look at each section separately, e.g., 60 ÷ 8 = 7.5. If one part is 6.5, it is short; if 8.5, it is long.

For proportions that may be out of balance, there are two methods of analysis. First, you look at each eighth to see if it is above the line (short) or below the line (long). This method, while simple, can be misleading. You're really better off dividing your height in inches by eight and then measuring each of the eighths on paper.

HOW DO YOU MEASURE UP?

Enter your measurements below, indicating if the measurement is short, long, or average.

Overall height _____ inches
Divided by eight _____ inches

	Inches	Short	Long	Average
Head to Neck	_____	_____	_____	_____
Neck to Bust	_____	_____	_____	_____
Bust to Waist	_____	_____	_____	_____
Waist to Hip	_____	_____	_____	_____
Hip to Thigh	_____	_____	_____	_____
Thigh to Knee	_____	_____	_____	_____
Knee to Calf	_____	_____	_____	_____
Calf to Sole	_____	_____	_____	_____

Look at the overall balance of your body, either looking in a mirror or using your front tracing. Draw a line (imaginary or otherwise) from the tip of your shoulder to the widest part of your hips (Figure 2-5).

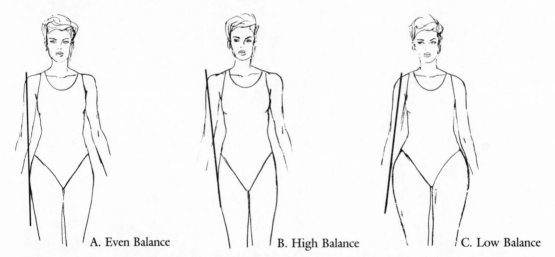

A. Even Balance   B. High Balance   C. Low Balance

Figure 2-5 *The angle between an imaginary line drawn from your shoulder tip to the widest part of your hips, reveals the balance of your body.*

- If the line is straight (A), you have an evenly balanced figure.
- If the line goes out at the shoulder (B), you have broad shoulders and/or narrow hips —a high-balanced figure.
- If the line goes out at the hip (C), you have a narrow shoulder and/or wide hips and thighs—a low-balanced figure.

We will explore figure balance more closely later on, but for now the following questions should clarify your figure type:

My shoulders are   narrow _____   broad _____   average _____
My figure balance is   even   _____   low _____   high   _____

The *slope* of your shoulder is measured in inches as the difference between the height of the tip of your shoulder and the height of the base of your neck (Figure 2-6).

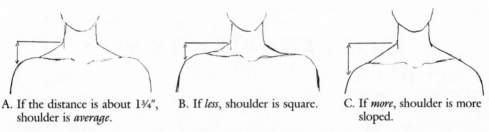

A. If the distance is about 1¾", shoulder is *average*.   B. If *less*, shoulder is square.   C. If *more*, shoulder is more sloped.

Figure 2-6 *Also look at the shoulder slope, which is the height difference between the neck base and shoulder tip.*

Using Figure 2-6, you can determine (either from your front tracing, or with the help of a friend) if your shoulders are:

square _____   sloped _____   average _____

Slope also refers to the pitch or tilt of your body from chin to knee. Certain physical traits such as a large high hip or a full and high derriere will tend to cause a garment to hike in the back (Figure 2-7).

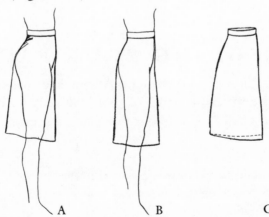

A   B   C

Figure 2-7 *A full rear, high hip, or very flat pelvis can make a skirt "slope" towards the front (A). To achieve the straight look (B), perform this shortening alteration (C), or have a tailor do it for you.*

Body slope frequently changes with weight gain and can change the fit of a garment, and if the weight is gained in the high hip or derriere, a given garment will probably require shortening in the front or lengthening in the back to avoid hiking in the back. If you have never had a problem with slope, and it becomes an issue on a given item, you may wish to hold out for another garment, as there still are some manufacturers who do not understand slope. Limit your purchases to manufacturers whose clothes show proven results of careful fit.

YOUR PROFILE TRAITS

If you did the profile tracing, you may wish to check for any of the following profile traits that tend to influence slope:

Jutting Chin	_____	Dowager's Hump	_____
Short Neck	_____	Long Neck	_____
Low Breasts	_____	High Breasts	_____
Full Bust	_____	Flat Bust	_____
Short Waist	_____	Long Waist	_____
Tummy Bulge	_____	Sway Back	_____
"Bubble Butt"*	_____	Full Derriere	_____

*A very full high back hip.

MEASURING YOUR FACE

Every face has unique features and proportions. A complete analysis of your physical self must include the most expressive eighth of your body (Figure 2-8).

Using Figure 2-8 as a guide, analyze your face using a mirror, a ruler, a piece of paper, and a pencil:

- Measure the distance from the top of your forehead to the bottom of your chin.
- Place a line of the same length on your paper and divide it horizontally in half and then in thirds, as in the illustration.
- Measure the widest part of your face, placing that horizontal line on your grid where it should be in relation to the length line.
- Begin to place your features where they fall according to your ruler.

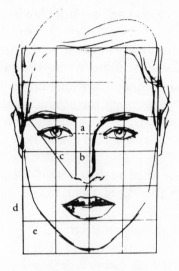

a. Should be one eye-width apart.

b. Nose corner and beginning of brow should form a straight line.

c. Nose corner to eye corner to brow end should form a straight line.

d. Cheekbone to jawline angle

e. Jawline to chin angle

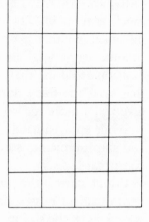

A. So-called perfect face   B. The real you

Figure 2-8

    According to image consultants the ideal face has a proportion of six in length to four in width, eyes that are one eye width apart, brows which begin in a straight angle with the corner of the nose and end at a 45° angle with the nose corner and the outside

FACE ANALYSIS

My face length is _____ inches	My face width is narrow	_____
My face width is _____ (at the widest part)	wide	_____
The widest part of my face is my _____	average	_____
My face shape is round _____	My eyes are small	_____
oval _____	average	_____
square _____	big	_____
rectangular _____	wide set	_____
diamond _____	narrow	_____
heart _____	My mouth is small	_____
pear _____	average	_____
My face length is short _____	large	_____
average _____	My chin is short	_____
long _____	average	_____
	long	_____
	strong	_____
	weak	_____

eye corner, and a smooth, gradual line from cheekbone to jawline, and from jawline to chin. Remember, we are not all Mona Lisas!

By now you may be yelling, "Stop!"—but I can tell you that you can never have too much fashion self-knowledge. One of our models tells of a fitting where the tailor informed her that her arms were about ¾″ shorter than average. Since then, she has become very conscious of her sleeve length, frequently shortening them. She says, "If he hadn't told me that, I never would have thought about it. . . . It's a little alteration that takes me from sloppy to polished." The information you are amassing here will give you a more realistic grasp on your true best sizes.

While approximately 25% of women qualify for petite sizes by their height, weight, and measurements, studies show that only 10% shop the Petite Departments on a consistent basis.

I think part of the problem is psychological—women usually wear one size larger in petite than in misses sizes, and in this day of *thin craziness*, many women are overly conscious of the size number. Further, many customers delude themselves that they are better off in misses sizes because they are not only numerically "thinner," but given more variety from which to choose.

Every year more "special size" (petite *or* large) women are buying clothes specially made for bodies like theirs. Look at the difference in this Bonnie Boerer misses-women's and petite top.

Look at the following charts and circle your proper sizes based on your measurements. There are three size-range charts: misses, petite, and women's petite.

MISSES SIZE CHART

Size	4	6	8	10	12	14	16	18	20	
Bust	33	34	35	36	38	39	40	42	44	Inches
Waist	23	24	25	26	28	29	30	32	34	Inches
Hips	33	34	35	36	38	40	42	43	45	Inches

PETITE SIZE CHART

Size	2P	4P	6P	8P	10P	12P	14P	16P	
Bust	32	33	34	35	36	38	39	41	Inches
Waist	22	23	24	25	26	28	29	31	Inches
Hips	33	34	35	36	37	38	40	41.5	Inches

WOMEN'S PETITE SIZE CHART

Size	12WP	14WP	16WP	18WP	20WP	22WP	24WP	26WP	
Bust	37	39	41	43	45	47	49	51	Inches
Waist	29	31	33	35	37	39	41	43	Inches
Hips	38	40	42	44	46	48	50	52	Inches

PETITE BODY MEASUREMENT CHART

Size	2P	4P	6P	8P	10P	12P	14P	
Bust	31	32	33	34	35	36.5	38	Inches
Waist	22	23	24	25.5	26.5	28	29	Inches
7″ Hip	33	34	35	36	37	38.5	40	Inches
Shoulder	14	14.25	14.5	14.75	15	15.25	15.5	Inches
Arm Length	21.25	21.5	21.75	22	22.25	22.5	22.75	Inches
Center Back Waist Length	15.25	15.5	15.75	16	16	16	16.25	Inches

Size	16WP	18WP	20WP	22WP	24WP	
Bust	40	42	44	46.5	49	Inches
Waist	31	33.5	35.5	38	40	Inches
7″ Hip	42	44	45	48.5	51	Inches
Shoulder	15.75	16	16.25	16.5	16.75	Inches
Arm Length	23.25	23.75	24	24.5	25	Inches
Center Back Waist Length	16.25	16.5	16.5	16.75	16.75	Inches

While some women fit perfectly into one size, more of us vary in size depending on where the snuggest part of the garment is. For example, a woman who measures 34-28-37 may wear an 8 petite or 6 misses blouse, 12 petite or 10 misses skirt, and 10 petite or 12 misses elastic-waist pant. So I suggest that you look at your sizes as a *range*.

	Petite	Misses
Bust Size	_____	_____
Waist Size	_____	_____
Hip Size	_____	_____

Let's visually examine the difference in misses and petite (Figures 2-9, 2-10, and 2-11):

Figure 2-9 Are you a petite or a misses customer? This illustration tells the whole story about the differences of proportion and construction in petite garments.

Figure 2-10 Look at the differences in proportion, scale, and design detail in these otherwise identical Bonnie Boerer tops.

Figure 2-11 Observe the size of stripes, prints, belts, and pleats in these garments, which have been designed by Taurus, a petite dress house with an eye for the very special needs of the petite customer, in proportion and scale.

I'm better off as an 8 petite, 5'3"—not as a short size 6 misses. How about you?

Keep in mind that petites are not all alike. Some are tiny, while others have misses sizing or larger sizes.

WHAT TYPE OF PETITE ARE YOU?

	Size												
	0	2	4	6	8	10	12	14	16	18	20	22	24+
4'9"	A	A	A	A	B	B	C	C	C	D	D	E	E
4'10"	A	A	A	B	B	B	C	C	C	D	D	E	E
4'11"	A	A	A	B	B	B	C	C	D	D	D	E	E
5'0"	A	A	B	B	B	C	C	D	D	D	E	E	E
5'1"	A	A	B	B	B	C	C	D	D	D	E	E	E
5'2"	A	A	B	B	B	C	C	D	D	E	E	E	E
5'3"	A	B	B	B	C	C	D	D	D	E	E	E	E
5'4"	A	B	B	C	C	C	D	D	D	E	E	E	E
5'5"*	B	B	C	C	D	D	D	D	D	E	E	E	E
5'6"*	B	B	C	C	D	D	D	D	D	E	E	E	E

*Many 5'5" and 5'6" women wear petite sizes to correct figure proportions, such as short waists, short legs or arms, or narrow shoulders or backs..

KEY

A	=	Diminutive
B	=	Small
C	=	Medium
D	=	Large
E	=	X-Large

Circle your height and usual size.

I am a _____ Petite.

3

THE ELEMENTS OF STYLE
COLOR, LINE AND FORM, AND TEXTURE

"You are small and frail and blue. Little sisters, I am, too."
—Dorothy Parker

Now that you have learned more about your individual physical traits, let's discuss the less tangible elements of personal style. These are:

1. Color, line and form, and texture
2. Body type
3. Personality and lifestyle
4. Proportion and scale

20

In this chapter, we will examine color, line and form, and texture. Once you learn how these elements can work for you, you will be able to put them together in your own special way to create the most flattering and "right" fashion profile for yourself.

COLOR

Color as it relates to fashion reflects my feeling about fashion in general: you can't know too much about either.

There are three elements to color (Figure 3-1):

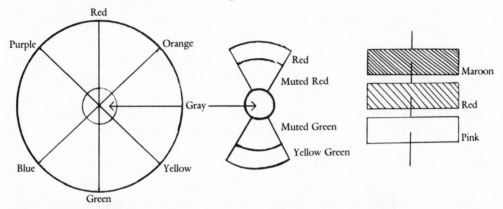

A. *Hue* refers to the position of the color on the color wheel; it is the actual name of the color, such as "red." Colors 180° apart on the wheel, such as red and green are called complementary colors.

B. *Intensity*, also called *clarity*, refers to the degree to which the color has been changed by the addition of its complementary color on the color wheel, e.g., red with a little green = muted red. Any two complementary colors added together in equal amounts will make gray.

C. *Value*, also called *depth*, reflects the degree of white or black which has been added to the hue. Hues with white added are called a *tint*; those with black added are called a *shade*, e.g., red with white = the tint pink; red with black = the shade maroon.

Figure 3-1

- Hue: Its name on the color wheel (*i.e.*, red, blue, yellow, etc.)
- Value: Its depth, darkness or lightness (*i.e.*, dark blue, light blue)
- Intensity: Purity, clarity, degree to which it is muted or not muted (*i.e.*, clear red is pure; dusty rose is muted)

Let's look at the color "Dusty Pink."

If you add pure white to pure red, you get a *value* of red called pink (pink is actually a tint of red, meaning a lighter value, where maroon would be a shade of red, meaning a darker value).

If you add some of the opposite color from the color wheel (green) to red, you get a more subdued, less intense form of red, called muted red, which is a muted intensity of red. Now, if you add white to muted red, you get a tint of red called dusty pink.

Colors that are 180° away from each other on the color wheel, are called **complementary colors**—not to be confused with complimentary colors, which means the ones that look good on you. Complementary colors tend to bring out the best in each other, too, which is why you see purple with yellow, blue with orange, red with green—they are all complements. Many major makeup artists will use complementary colors for dazzling eye makeup effects—roses on green eyes, orange-bronze on blue eyes, and lavender on brown eyes.

Color tells a great deal about you:

- The colors you **wear** show how you feel about yourself, how you want others to perceive you and what you think looks good on you; *i.e.*, navy may mean you wish to appear conservative and neat, and think you look best in dark tones.
- The colors you use in your **home** show what you feel you lack or what you need in your environment; *e.g.*, blue walls may mean you crave peace and rest.

There are two ways of perceiving color: **connotation**—your rational knowledge of color; *i.e.*, its name and components; and **denotation**—your emotional response to color, based on a lifetime of experiences; *i.e.*, you broke your arm when you were five, chasing a big red balloon, and to this day you think of red as a wild and dangerous color.

Y O U R   C O L O R   R E S P O N S E

ere's a list of popular colors with some common denotations. Circle those which apply to you, and add your own:

Red	Passionate, sexual, aggressive, energetic, bloody, angry, vital, exciting
White	Clean, pure, young, bland, safe
Black	Simple, severe, mysterious, sophisticated, sexy, glum, depressing, deadly
Orange	Fruity, happy, unique, new, motivated, garish, hot
Green	Fresh, new, growing, successful, loving, envious, greedy
Yellow	Sunny, optimistic, joyful, clear, positive, cowardly, ill
Purple	Royal, grown-up, rich, passionate, sexy, alone

Blue	Calming, cool, quiet, sleepy, sad
Brown	Warm, earthy, safe, drab
Gray	Mature, subtle, dignified, gloomy, glum, cold
Pink	Soft, innocent, feminine, silly
Hot Pink	Wild, sensual, daring, flashy, vulgar

How Do You Know Which Colors to Wear?

Carole Jackson wrote a book in 1980 based on seasonal color theory called *Color Me Beautiful*. Four million copies have been sold, many to women who use the book to analyze themselves, while others use professional color analysts and image consultants. I highly recommend using an image consultant, if you can afford one, as a good image consultant can improve your color sense, saving you lots of money in the long run.

Carole Jackson has provided us with some very useful information for *The Complete Petite*. The most asked question in color analysis is, why do it in the first place?

The seasonal colors of Spring, Summer, Winter, or Fall give a set of guidelines for a harmonious and flattering palette, which, in turn, tends to blend within itself, making your clothes more versatile, easier to accessorize, and virtually mistake-proof. Working within seasonal parameters (within reason) makes the process of wardrobe building and buying cosmetics and accessories easier.

To be sure of your personal color season, either find a professional analyst, who will "drape" you in big swatches of different colors, or ask friends who can be objective.

Finding Your Color "Season"

To determine, as best you can, your color season, try this test. The following *key colors* are colors most likely to succeed in any given season. Circle the colors below which you feel to be your best, **not just O.K., but your best**. You will find that you have a majority of circles in one season, but if you don't, I've included a tie-breaker.

KEY COLORS

COOL TONES	WARM TONES
(You look best in blue-base colors)	(You look best in gold colors)
Winter Colors	**Spring Colors**
(Bright and Bold)	(Bright and Lively)
Red	Coral
Royal Blue	Bright Periwinkle

(Continued)

KEY COLORS (Continued)

COOL TONES	WARM TONES
(You look best in blue-base colors)	(You look best in gold colors)

Winter Colors	Spring Colors
Purple	Turquoise
Fuchsia	Coral Pink
White	Camel
Emerald Green	Kelly Green
Navy	Light True Blue
Ice Pink	Peach

Summer Colors	Autumn Colors
(Grayed and Soft)	(Muted and Dark)
Red	Tomato Red
Baby Blue	Rust
Baby Pink	Gold
Lavender	Deep Peach
Mauve	Deep Lavender
Blue Green	Forest Green
Cadet Gray Blue	Teal Blue
Wine	Brown

The following simplified quiz will help to make you more certain:

- **Winter**: Think clear colors and contrast. Are *black* and *white* among your very best colors?
- **Summer**: Think soft, cool, slightly grayed colors. Are *pink* and *baby blue* among your very best colors?
- **Spring**: Think bright, fresh colors. Are *coral* and *camel* among your very best colors?
- **Autumn**: Think deep, muted colors. Are *rust* and *brown* among your very best colors?

Remember, you are only one season. Use that season to always look your best. Once you know your colors, you can use color to dress better. For example, many women wear a lot of black, thinking that it will make them look taller and thinner. But if black is not one of your best colors, it will only make you look tired and older. Only wear your best colors, especially next to your face (Figure 3-2).

Solid colors tend to make you look thinner and taller, especially when the same color is worn from head to toe (monochromatic dressing). Dividing the body into numerous

Figure 3-2 White is more expansive than black.

color blocks can shorten and widen the body, which is not as much a problem to slim petites as it is to heavy petites. To look taller and slimmer, avoid big prints and stick to solid colors, which tend to be more flattering and have a longer fashion life, as prints often date quickly (Figure 3-3).

Figure 3-3 Monochromatic dressing is more slimming and elongating than dressing in contrasting color blocks or pattern blocks.

Once you have determined your season, you should become familiar with your best colors. There are many books on this subject, and many professional color analysts and sources for color analysis. Some guidelines for your seasons are listed below. If you are still unsure of your season, check off the colors which you think are best for you; perhaps you will be able to decide.

	Cool		Warm	
	Winter	Summer	Spring	Autumn
	clear	soft	bright	muted
Black	Black	—	—	—
White	Blue White	Soft White	Ivory	Oyster
Gray	Silver Charcoal Icy Gray Charcoal Blue	Silver Blue Gray Light Blue Gray	Warm Gray Light Warm Gray Clear Gray	Pewter Gray Green
Beige	Light Taupe	Rose Beige	Warm Beige Camel Golden Tan	Warm Beige Camel Buff
Brown	Dark Chocolate Brown	Cocoa Rose Brown	Medium Golden Brown Dark Golden Brown	Bronze Mahogany Dark Chocolate Rust
Red	Blue Red Burgundy True Red	Soft Red Wine Blue Red Watermelon	Red Orange Clear, Bright Red Tomato Red	Burgundy Orange Red Dark Tomato Red
Yellow	Ice Yellow Lemon Yellow	Pale Lemon	Buff Chamois Golden Yellow Light Gold	Gold Golden Yellow Light Gold Buff
Green	Ice Green Clear Green Emerald	Teal Spruce Blue Green	Light Clear Green Light Yellow Green	Yellow Green Forest Khaki

(Continued)

	Cool		Warm	
	Winter	Summer	Spring	Autumn
	clear	soft	bright	muted
	Dark Green	Pale Blue-Green	Medium Yellow Green Kelly Green Chartreuse Light Teal	Jade Olive
Blue	Ice Blue Royal True Blue Periwinkle Navy Chinese Blue	Gray Navy Cadet Blue Periwinkle Medium Blue Pale Blue Powder Blue	Light True Blue Light Clear Navy Periwinkle Medium Blue Dark Periwinkle	Teal Deep Periwinkle
Aqua	Turquoise Bright Blue-Green Ice Aqua	Pale Aqua Medium Aqua	Green Turquoise Light Warm Aqua Medium Warm Aqua	Medium Aqua Dark Aqua Turquoise
Purple	Magenta Fuchsia Royal Purple Ice Violet	Soft Fuchsia Lavender Orchid Plum Violet Raspberry	Medium Violet	Purple Eggplant
Pink	Ice Pink Hot Pink	Pastel Pink Rose Deep Rose Mauve Azalea	Peach Pink Coral Pink Bright Warm Pink	Salmon Pink
Orange	—	—	Orange Red Light Orange Salmon Coral Peach	Brick Pumpkin Bright Orange Salmon Apricot Light Peach

Color is an important factor in style, but there are other elements, too. Let's explore them.

LINE AND FORM

Line and form are the most important words in fashion. **Form** refers to the outside shape or silhouette of a garment. **Line** refers to what goes on within the form. For example, a chemise shirt dress has a rectangular form with a vertical line formed by front and center plackets, and a horizontal line formed by a belt.

To understand line and form, study Figures 3-4 through 3-9.

A. The *form* of the garment is trapeze; the *line* inside the form is horizontal.

B. The ball is round in *form*; the *line* inside the form is zigzag.

Figure 3-4

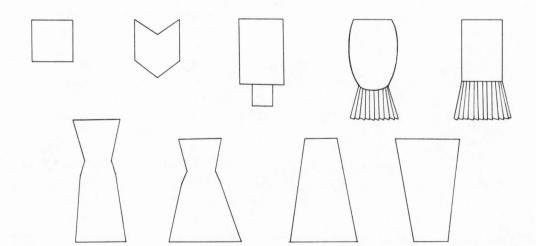

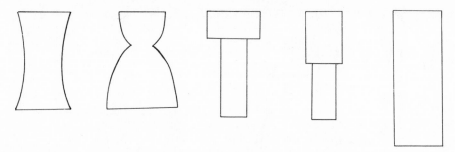

Figure 3-5 Forms in fashion are only **somewhat** limited by the female body.

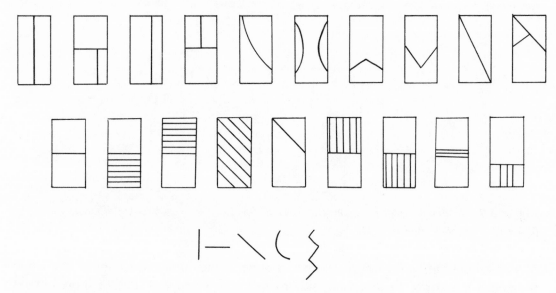

Figure 3-6 Possible lines *are more varied than forms in fashion; these are only a few.*

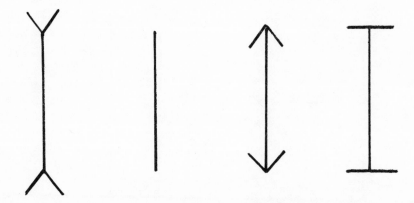

Figure 3-7 All of the above vertical lines are the same height, but some seem taller or shorter.

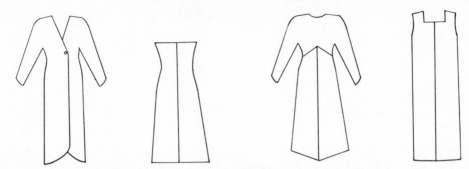

Figure 3-8 *Which of these dresses will make you look tallest and thinnest? The first dress is the most elongating, the second dress is the least.*

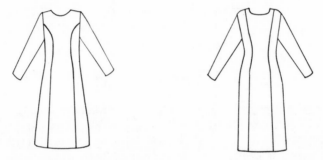

Figure 3-9 *The slight change in the princess lines of these two dresses make a big difference—the first dress seems wider and shorter.*

Vertical lines make the eye travel up and down, which slim and elongate you, while horizontal lines draw the eye from side to side and widen you. Petites should avoid extreme oversized forms. Any garment should fit without being tight or without having a lot of extra fabric (Figure 3-10).

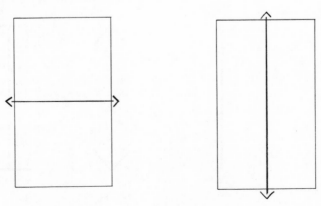

Figure 3-10 *Horizontal lines widen and shorten and vertical lines slim and elongate.*

TEXTURE

Texture affects a garment in two ways: it thins or widens. Shiny, heavy, and/or rough fabrics add thickness. Matte and soft fabrics drape and contour.

Texture can improve or detract from your appearance. It has three elements:

- **Feel**: Smooth, soft, hard, rough
- **Weight**: Light, medium, heavy
- **Shine**: Shiny, glossy, matte

Review the following **texture** chart:

Texture	Elongates	Slims	Shortens	Widens	Mood
Feel					
Rough			X	X	Earthy
Hard			X	X	Formal
Smooth	X	X			Elegant
Soft	X	X			Feminine
Weight					
Thick			X	X	Sturdy
Medium	——————————— varies ———————————				Conservative
Light	X	X			Soft
Shine					
Shiny				X	Bright
Semigloss	——————————— varies ———————————				Fresh
Matte	X	X			Classic

Texture may be affected by trim and detail, such as buttons, braids, pleats, appliqués, and embroideries. A soft, matte sheath dress takes on a very different look when it has large buttons, bold braid, and vast areas of appliqué.

Now that you know all about color, line and form, and texture,
let's go on to your body "type" and the fashions that are
best for you.

4

THE ELEMENTS OF STYLE
BODY TYPE

Understanding your **body type** will help you make the right fashion choices. While Carole Jackson wrote the book on color, Mary Duffy, my co-author, wrote the book on body type: The *H-O-A-X Fashion Formula*. Mary believes that women make the worst fashion mistakes when they choose garments because of the way they appear on models or friends, with little or no consideration of their own particular build. Any quest for fashion self-knowledge must include a careful examination of one's own body type.

There are four body types, "H," "O," "A," and "X." Used properly, the **HOAX** theory will teach you to dress your figure flatteringly, boosting your confidence and self-image. The **HOAX** theory will show you how to:

- Emphasize your best figure points
- De-emphasize the parts of your body which you consider less than wonderful.

The first rule of **H-O-A-X** is: Think of yourself as having a figure type, not figure flaws, with a combination of good and not-so-good traits. Here are the four body types (Figure 4-1):

H A straight up-and-down shape

O A full torso, thin legs and thigh shape

A A bottom-heavy or hip-and-thigh-heavy shape

X A curvy hourglass shape

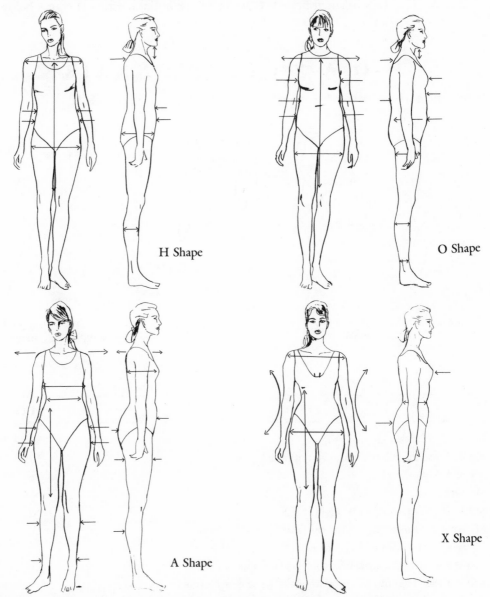

H Shape

O Shape

A Shape

X Shape

Figure 4-1 *The four body types from front and profile views. The arrows indicate (by direction) visual illusions of emphasis or de-emphasis which are generally desired for each body type.*

Here are the similarities and differences of each body type:

H & O	Figures without much (or any) waist
A & X	Figures with clearly defined, indented waists.
H & X	Evenly proportioned figures with a 2″ or less difference in bust and hip (bust is the smaller). **H** has a straighter rib cage and wider waist.
O & A	Less balanced figures. **O** is bigger **above** the waist. **A** is bigger **below** the waist.

H-O-A-X QUESTIONNAIRE

Circle the correct answer for your body as it looks *now* (Figure 4-2)!

A. Indented waistline

B. Straight or wide waistline

C. Wide high hip (square hip)

D. Full mid-hip (rounded hip)

E. Full front thigh line (saddle bag hip)

Figure 4-2

	H-O	A-X
My back and shoulders are fleshy.	Yes	No
My back and shoulders are firm and smooth.	No	Yes
My neck is short and full.	Yes	No
My neck is average or long.	No	Yes
My arms and legs tend to be fleshy.	No	Yes
My arms and legs tend to be proportionally slender and shapely.	Yes	No
I have a clearly indented waistline (a).	No	Yes
I have a straight ribcage and a proportionally wide (or nonexistent) waistline (b).	Yes	No
I have a wide high hip and proportionally average or narrow thighs (c).	Yes	No
I have wide hips, widest at the mid-hip or thigh.	No	Yes

If you are tied (5 **H-O** circles, 5 **A-X** circles), you are probably an **H** or an **X**, so complete both **H-O** and **A-X** sections, paying most attention to the questions about the waist. (A small waist and round hip = **X**; a straight waist and square hip = **H**.) Otherwise, proceed to the section—**H-O** or **A-X**—where you have the most circles.

Determining whether you are an **H** or an **O**:

	H	O
My thighs are the narrowest part of my torso.	No	Yes
I have a tendency to a slight thigh bulge.	Yes	No
I have tiny ankles supporting a big torso.	No	Yes
My torso has a straight, squarish look.	Yes	No
From the side view, my bust, midriff, or tummy is particularly protuberant.	No	Yes
My bust is bigger than my hips or thighs.	No	Yes
I have a short neck and a dowager's hump.	No	Yes
I have an extremely full face for my overall size.	No	Yes
My hips and bust are even.	Yes	No

Determining whether you are an **A** or an **X**

	A	X
My shoulders are noticeably narrower than my hips and thighs.	Yes	No
My bust is noticeably narrower than my hips and thighs.	Yes	No
My bust and hips are even (within 0–2″ difference).	No	Yes
My hips are round and fullest at the mid-hip (d).	No	Yes
My hips are fullest at the front thigh line (e).	Yes	No
I have an even bust and hips and a small waist.	No	Yes
My figure is an hourglass.	No	Yes

Now that you have determined your body type, here are the best ways for you to dress in order to present yourself to best advantage.

BODY TYPE "H"

If you are an **H**, you should:

1. Create the illusion of a more indented waist.
2. Distract from your mid-section, and bring attention to your mid-hip, thighs, and legs.

3. De-emphasize a squarish or heavy back, back waist, and/or high hip.
4. Elongate with predominantly vertical lines.

Figure 4-3   A. Styles that are good on an "H."

Your **best** wardrobe choices are (Figure 4-3A):

Dresses	Tops
2-Piece Dresses	Overblouses
Blousons	Camisoles
Dropped Waists	Skimps
Fanny Wraps	Cowls
Cocoons	Shells
Chemises	Cardigans
A-Lines	Sailors
Sheaths	Notched/Convertible Collars

Bottoms	Coats and Jackets
Straight Skirts	Chesterfields/Polo Coats
Crystal Pleats	Dusters
Godets/Trumpets	Reefers
Soft Modified Dirndls	Tuxedos
Straight/Peg Pants	Fly-Aways
Leggings/Stirrups	Blazers
Shorts	Strollers
Pleated Trousers	Battle Jackets

Undies	Swimsuits
Body Briefers	Maillots
Full Slips	Tanks
Split Petticoats	Blousons
Camisoles	French Cuts
Longline Bras	Halters
Shoulder Pads	Sarongs

Miscellaneous	
Elasticized Belts	V-Necks
Long Beads/Pearls	Long Scarves

The **worst** wardrobe choices for an **H** are (Figure 4-3B):

Figure 4-3   B. Styles that are bad for an "H."

Dresses	Tops
Set-In Waists	Turtlenecks
Wraps	Polos
Tents	Surplices
Smocks	Horizontal Stripes

Bottoms	Coats and Jackets
Circle Skirts	Boleros
Kilts/Box Pleat Skirts	Waistcoats
Bell Bottom Pants	Balmacaans
Harem Pants	Swagger Coats

BODY TYPE "O"

If you are an **O**, you should:

1. Make your waist appear more indented.
2. Draw the eye away from the middle and upper torso and to the hips, thighs, and legs.
3. De-emphasize fullness in the shoulders, neck, and face.
4. Create vertical lines to draw the eye up and down and to create the illusion of top and bottom balance.

Your **best** wardrobe choices are (Figure 4-4A):

Figure 4-4   A. Styles that are good on an "O."

Dresses	Tops
Blousons	Blousons
Fanny Wraps	Sailor Collars
Chemises	Cardigans
Floats	V-Necks

(Continued)

Dresses	Tops
Bubbles	Overblouses
Jackets	Cowl Necks
Dropped Waists	Notched Collars
2-Piece Overblouses	Skimps

Bottoms	Coats and Jackets
Straight Skirts	Capes
Elastic-Waist Skirts/Pants	Polos/Overcoats
Godet/Trumpet Skirts	Tabard Vests
Capri Pants	Dusters
Shorts	Smocks
Stirrup/Legging Pants	Strollers
Short Skirts	Flings
Cropped Pants	Ponchos

Undies	Swimsuits
Body Briefers	Maillots
Longline Bras	Boy Legs
Underwire Bras	V-Necks
Full Slips	Sarongs
Camisoles/Split Pettis	Tanks
Shoulder Pads	Blousons

Miscellaneous	
Elasticized Belts	Long Beads/Pearls
2″ Heels	Long Scarves

Your **worst** wardrobe choices are (Figure 4-4B):

Dresses	Tops
Set-In Waists	High Necks
Strapless	Halters
Tents	Sweater Vests
Surplices	Turtlenecks

Figure 4-4   B. Styles that are bad for an "O."

Bottoms	Coats and Jackets
Jeans	Wrap Coats
Jumpsuits/Rompers	Trench Coats
Bell Bottoms	Boleros
Pleated Trousers	Blazers

BODY TYPE "A"

If you are an **A**, you should:

1. Emphasize a small waist and graceful neck and back.
2. Broaden a narrow shoulder and the upper torso.
3. De-emphasize the hip, derriere, and thigh.
4. Create the illusion of top and bottom balance.

Your **best** wardrobe choices are (Figure 4-5A):

Dresses	Tops
Set-In Waists	Ruffle Fronts
Surplices	Turtlenecks
Strapless	High Necks
Sundresses	Polos
Empires	Button Downs

(Continued)

Figure 4-5   A. Styles that are good on an "A."

Dresses	Tops
Tents	Sweater Vests
Princess	Crew Necks
A-Lines	Sweatshirts

Bottoms	Coats and Jackets
Pleated Trousers	Balmacaans
Skorts	Trenches
Dropped-Waist (Yokes)	Swaggers
Palazzos	Semi-Fitted
A-Lines	Boleros
Gathered/Dirndls	Peplums
Circles	Blazers
Pleats (thin fabrics only)	Spencer/Norfolk

Undies	Swimsuits
Control Top Pantyhose	Maillots
Capri Girdles	Surplices
Padded Bras	Skirted
T-Shirts	Sarongs
Half Slips	French Cuts
Shoulder Pads	Dressmaker

Miscellaneous	
Belts	Scarves
Full Sleeves	Necklaces

Your **worst** wardrobe choices are (Figure 4-5B):

Figure 4-5   B. Styles that are bad for an "A."

Dresses	Tops
Knit Sheaths	Blousons
Fanny Wraps	Skimps
Blousons	Halters
Bubbles	Overblouses

Bottoms	Coats and Jackets
Leggings	Polos
Straight	Reefers
Shorts	Strollers
Capri	Tabards

BODY TYPE "X"

If you are an **X**, you should:

1. Call attention to the waist.
2. De-emphasize the full bust.
3. Emphasize the soft curve of the hipline.
4. Show off the curvy balance of the figure with draping and softness.

Your **best** wardrobe choices are (Figure 4-6A):

Figure 4-6   A. Styles that are good on an "X."

Dresses	Tops
Sheaths	Bows
Dropped Waists	Cardigans
Strapless	T-Shirts
Coat Dresses	Cowls
Shirtdresses	Surplices
Chemises	Halters
Sundresses	Tanks
A-Lines	Cossacks

Bottoms	Coats and Jackets
Trousers	Balmacaans
Leggings	Dusters
Gauchos	Blazers
Straight Pants and Skirts	Tuxedos
Jeans	Trenches
Shorts	Strollers
Dirndl Skirts	Peplums
Pleated Skirts	

Undies	Swimsuits
Full Slips	2-Pieces
Underwire Bras	Maillots
Control Briefs	Halters
Control Top Pantyhose	Bikinis
Camisoles	Tanks
Shoulder Pads	Strapless

Miscellaneous	
Belts	Scarves
Cinched Waists	Shawls

Your **worst** wardrobe choices are (Figure 4-6B):

Dresses	Tops
Bubbles	Skimps
Blousons	Overblouses
Floats	Ruffle Fronts
Peasants	Sailor Collars

Bottoms	Coats and Jackets
Palazzos	Tabard Vests
Tube Skirts	Fly-Aways
Wide Shorts	Smocks
Slit Skirts	Fluffy Jackets

Figure 4-6   B. Styles that are bad for an "X."

Here are some more style hints to help you to de-emphasize less flattering portions of your anatomy.

FIGURE TRAIT CORRECTION CHART

Characteristics	Dresses and Tops (Including Necklines and Collars)	Bottoms: Skirts and Pants
Double Chin Short Neck	Sailor, Winged, Teardrop, Shawl, Chelsea, Scoop, Deep "U," Off-Shoulder V-neck, Strapless, Long/ Pointed Collars *Avoid high necks, small scarves, chokers, and neck bows.*	
Narrow or Sloping Shoulders	Padded Shoulders, Diagonal Stripes, Square Necklines, Batteau, Smocked, Western, Wide Collars, Sailor, Winged, Pleated, Capped, or Epaulet Shoulders, Pushed-Up Sleeves, Peasant Look	(Continued)

FIGURE TRAIT CORRECTION CHART (Continued)

Characteristics	Dresses and Tops (Including Necklines and Collars)	Bottoms: Skirts and Pants
	Avoid anything with soft or sloped shoulders, V- or U-necklines,* strapless and camisoles, as well as anything off the shoulder.	
Wide Shoulders	Peplum Dresses, Deep "U," Square Necks, Bib, Ascot, Teardrop, Notched, Shawl, Chelsea, Bishop/ Raglan Sleeves, Set-In Sleeves	Full Skirt and Full Pant Silhouettes
	Avoid cap sleeves and shoulder pads.	*Avoid narrow skirts and pants.*
Dowager's Hump	Portrait Necklines, Yoked Collars with Gathers, Collars That Stand Up	
	Avoid low backs, boat necks, strapless or spaghetti straps, and sleeveless garments.	
Thin Arms	Long Sleeve and Full Sleeve Treatments, Bishop Sleeves, Classic Shirtwaists, Short Cuffed Sleeves, Cardigans, Sweatshirts	
	Avoid strapless, halter, sleeveless, tank, long vertical necklines, snug knits, and clingy fabrics.	
Heavy Arms	Loose or Full Sleeves such as Dolman, Kimono, Bishop, Classic Sleeves, T-Shaped Sundresses, Wedge Dresses, Padded Shoulders, Any Detail Giving Attention to Neckline	
	Avoid puffy sleeves, very snug sleeves, sleeveless, and horizontal stripes.	

(Continued)

*Unless worn with shoulder pads.

FIGURE TRAIT CORRECTION CHART (Continued)

Characteristics	Dresses and Tops (Including Necklines and Collars)	Bottoms: Skirts and Pants
Big Bust	V-Necks, Small Shoulder Pads, Unbelted Soft Lines, Sweetheart Necklines, Blouson Styles	Narrow Waistbands
	Avoid clingy fabrics, belted set-in waists, and empire.	*Avoid wide waistbands and soft pleats.*
Flat Bust	Set-In Waists, Blousons, Dropped Waists, Empire Waists, Layered Looks, Light Colors on Top, Padded, Capped, Puffed, Wide Collars, Ruffle Fronts	Straight, A-Line
	Avoid princess, sheath, open necks, and strapless.	*Don't make lower body appear too large, making the bust appear smaller.*
Long Waist	A-Line Dresses and Separates, Princess, Empire, Dropped Waists, Chemises, Set-In, Wide, and Long Sleeves, Wide Necklines, Boleros	High Rise, Palazzo, Stirrups *Avoid straight, yoke and short skirts, and horizontal stripes on bottom.*
Short Waist	Blouson, Princess, Empire, Chemise, Dropped Waists, Vertical Neckline	Shortish Skirts (Mid-Calf), Slimmer Skirts with Longer Skirts, Culottes, Knickers
	Avoid set-in waist, 2-piece dressing, bolero, big sleeves, and wide, big necklines.	*Avoid high rise and palazzo.*
Thick or Wide Waist	Blouson, Dropped Waists, Chemise, Dresses with No Waist, Long Tops, Loose Fitting Tops, Tops That Hit Hipline	Full Leg Trousers, Flared Skirts, Narrow or Moderate Width Skirts, Stirrup Pants
	Avoid set-in waists, bolero, crop, tube, halter, and wrap.	*Avoid full skirts and pleated pants.*

(Continued)

FIGURE TRAIT CORRECTION CHART (Continued)

Characteristics	Dresses and Tops (Including Necklines and Collars)	Bottoms: Skirts and Pants
Big Tummy	Waistless Dress, Blouson, Empire, Chemise, Wrap Dresses with Diagonal Closing, Overblouses and Tunics, Loose Sweaters and Blouses	Full Cut Pants or Culottes, Modified Dirndls, Semi-Fitted, Eased Fronts, Pleated Trousers, A-Line Skirts
	Avoid clingy fabrics and sheaths, bolero, crop, and halter tops.	*Avoid narrow skirts.*
Big Hips and Derriere	Set-In Waists, Full Skirts, A-Lines, Princess, Tent, Collarless Straight Jackets to Skim Skirts, Full Shapes, Broad Shoulders, and Heavy Sweaters.	Wrap Skirts, Slightly Gathered Dirndls, A-Line Culottes, Pleated Trousers
	Avoid sheaths, chemises, dropped waists, fanny wraps, T-shirts, tank tops, camisoles, and halters.	*Avoid narrow skirts, leggings, and stirrup pants.*
Narrow Hips and Derriere	Fanny Wraps, Dropped Waists, Chemises, Set-In Waists, Full Skirts, A-Line, Princess, Tents, Overblouses, Tunics	Narrow Skirts, Legging Stirrup Pants, Pants with Pleats
	Avoid poor boy, turtleneck, and bolero	
Heavy Legs	Vertical Lines, Loose Fitted Dresses, Long Tunics, Well-Tailored Dresses with Good Seam Allowances, Padded Shoulders with Epaulettes, Puffed, Peasant Look, Kimonos, Dolman Sleeves, Raglans, Halters, Peplums	Wide Leg Pants, Straight Leg Pants, Dropped Waist Circular Skirts, Dirndls and Modified Dirndls, Stitched Pleats, Knife Pleats, Wraps
		Avoid straight, flared, sarong, 8-gore hip huggers, and wide leg shorts.
Thin Legs		Dirndls, Open Pleating, Tapered, Sarong, A-Lines, Culottes, Flared Leg Trousers, Jogging/Warm-Up Pants

(Continued)

FIGURE TRAIT CORRECTION CHART (Continued)

Characteristics	Outerwear and Jackets	Lingerie, Swimwear, and Miscellaneous
		Avoid tiered, flounced, tights, and stirrup pants.
Double Chin Short Neck	1-Button Jackets, Blazers, Tuxedo Coats, Tunic Vests, Bolero, Weskit, Cardigan Look	Vertical Lines in Clothing, Long Chains, 1-Color Dressing, Move Focal Point Away from Chin
		Avoid long, dangling earrings.
Narrow or Sloping Shoulders	Padded Shoulders, 3/4 Length Jackets, Field Jackets, Coachman, Sherlock Holmes, Safari, Trenches, Pea Coats	Shoulder Pads, Camisoles, Shoulder Pads, T-Shirts, Halters, Strapless, Deep-Cut Armholes, Wide Thick Straps
Wide Shoulders	Double-Breasted Open Blazers, Asymmetrical Coats, Car Coats, Chesterfields, Balmacaans	Halter and Thin Straps, Necklaces and Scarves
	Avoid ponchos, cocoons, and shawls.	*Avoid strapless and epaulettes.*
Dowager's Hump	Loose Fitting Coats, Jackets	Racer Back, Be Conscious of Posture
	Avoid ponchos, shawls, and cocoons.	*Avoid low-tying scarf treatments, chokers, and long necklines.*
Thin Arms	Parkas, Shawls, Cuffs and Buttons at Wrist to Draw Eye Downward, Bombardier Style Jackets, Fur Collars, Short Jackets	Small Hand and Wrist Jewelry *Avoid spaghetti straps, strapless, halters, and big hand jewelry.*
Heavy Arms	Shawls, Light Fabrics, Ponchos, Cocoons	Draping Slit Sleeves on Nightwear
	Avoid heavy fabrics, parkas, coachman, and Sherlock Holmes.	*Avoid camisoles, empire swimsuits, and oversized rings and bracelets.*

(Continued)

FIGURE TRAIT CORRECTION CHART (Continued)

Characteristics	Outerwear and Jackets	Lingerie, Swimwear, and Miscellaneous
Big Bust	Unstructured Jackets, Tunic Vests, Open Blazers, Loose Soft Styles, Cape Coats or Jackets with Fullness	Minimizer Bras (**A well-fitted bra is a necessity!**), Narrow Belts, Use 1-Tone Dressing with Darker Tops
	Avoid anything fitted, double breasted, and empire waist.	*Avoid gaping buttons and wide belts.*
Flat Busts	Belted, Double Breasted Short Wrap Jackets	Padded Bras, **Accessories are a must!**
	Avoid princess and anything fitted.	*Avoid push-up bras and scarves.*
Long Waist	Short Jackets, Double Breasted	Match Belt to Bottom, Control Top, Blousons, Let Point of Bust Drop Slightly, 2-Piece Maillots with Horizontal Band of Color at Waist
	Avoid boleros and short, fitted jackets.	*Avoid lengthening by matching top, skimpy bikinis and low-hip panties.*
Short Waist	Semi-Fitted Jackets, Unbelted Tunics	Bras That Uplift Breasts, Blouson or Straight Leg Swimsuits, Belts Matching Top
	Avoid fitted, short jackets ending at waist	*Avoid letting bust sag, bold contrast at waist, belts matching bottom, and 2-piece or high-cut leg swimsuits.*
Heavy Waist	Long Jackets, Full Coats	Waist Cinchers, Body Briefers, Bras That Keep Bust High, Blousons, 1-Color Looks
	Avoid fitted jackets and coats and anything double breasted.	*Avoid panty girdles, 2-piece bathing suits, thick belts, and big handbags.*
Big Tummy	Long and Full Coats, Chanel, Blazers, Cardigans	Panty Girdles, Body Briefers, Control Top Pantyhose, "Flatter Front" or Blouson Swimsuits, Dark Belts

(Continued)

FIGURE TRAIT CORRECTION CHART (Continued)

Characteristics	Outerwear and Jackets	Lingerie, Swimwear, and Miscellaneous
	Avoid anything fitted, short, or bolero.	*Avoid bikini pants, hip belts, and 2-piece swimsuits.*
Big Hips and Derriere	Fly-Away jackets, A-Lines, Full Coats	Control Top Pantyhose, Thigh Girdles, French Leg Swimsuits, Padded Shoulders
	Avoid short jackets and straight coats.	*Avoid hip-emphasizing accessories and straight-leg bathing suits.*
Narrow Hips and Flat Derriere	Hip-Length Jackets, Slim Coats	Body Briefers, Blousons, Sarongs, Hip Belts
	Avoid full and A-line coats.	*Avoid tank swimsuits.*
Heavy Legs	Parkas, Coach with Large Collar, Sherlock Holmes, Trenches, Cardigans, Shawls, Capes, Tents, Loosely Fitted Jackets	Empire Waists, Boxer or Wide Bottom Briefs, Hosiery to Match Shoes and Hemline, Pinstripe- or Vertical-Stripe Hosiery, V-Cut Leg Swimsuit, Accessories to Draw Eye above Waist
	Avoid high rise briefs, light-colored hose, and leg warmers.	*Avoid straight-cut leg swimsuit.*
Thin Legs	Chesterfields, Balmacaans	Colored or Textured Pantyhose, Boxer Style Briefs, Straight-Cut Leg Swimsuits
		Avoid ruffled or tiered skirts.

After absorbing all of this basic information on color, line, form, texture, and body type, you can use your newfound knowledge to determine what fashions and fabrics best suit you.

Let's move on to the aspects of **lifestyle** and **personality**.

5

THE ELEMENTS OF STYLE
LIFESTYLE AND PERSONALITY

"Exuberance is better than taste."
—GUSTAVE FLAUBERT, 1869

Let's look at you—the real woman within. As color, body type, proportion define the external you, that less easily understood trait **style** is defined by the internal you. A "woman of style" knows who she is, projects uniqueness to others, and wears clothes well because she chooses them to suit both her personality and her lifestyle.

Two women greatly influenced my love of style. One is my mother, who grew up in New York, Paris, and Italy, where she was exposed to the finest clothes made. Her wedding dress was made for her by Worth in Paris. She was often photographed by roving photographers from magazines and newspapers in Europe and the United States.

A favorite photo of mine shows Mom in Palm Beach, caught unaware, with a shy, startled look, wearing a T-shirt and striped pants. The caption reads: "Simone Attwood wearing the new French cotton pants." Today, Mom is a size 6 petite. Her closet contains everything from Patou dresses, Chanel suits, and vintage Anne Klein suits to Calvin Klein denims. Looking good, Mom!

Great aunt Hazel is my other role model. Winner of the Paris Gold Medal in ballroom dancing during the 1920s, she was one of the first women in Paris to wear trousers. They were made of gold lamé and worn under a silk organdy seafoam green dress, so that they glimmered through. Reed thin, with thick dark hair and a flawless complexion, she was often photographed about town by *Vogue* magazine, once with a captioned request for "the mystery woman" to contact them and divulge her dressmakers. Hazel actually designed and created her clothes herself. Today, in her late eighties, her face and figure lovely and well cared for, her style sense is thoroughly modern—no granny dresses or mismatched dowdy outfits for her!

Style is hard to define. It is not the same as taste, which is entirely subjective. Neither is it based on buying expensive designer labels. Like real friendship, style cannot be bought. It can only be learned or developed over time. Some women who rely on pricey items to create an image often look as though the clothes are wearing them, not the other way around! Style comes from an understanding of yourself—how you approach the way you look, feel, and live.

Style is projecting your uniqueness, and **taste** is knowing what's appropriate, and **sex appeal** is having innate femaleness. For fun and for a highlighted "fashion" awareness, rate the following women:

	Style	Taste	Sex Appeal
Audrey Hepburn			
Katherine Hepburn			
Lauren Bacall			
Elizabeth Taylor			
Dolly Parton			
Princess Diana			
Angela Lansbury			
Farrah Fawcett			
Lena Horne			
Greta Garbo			
Goldie Hawn			
Liza Minnelli			
Iman			
Gloria Vanderbilt			
Paloma Picasso			
Diana Ross			
Jane Pauley			
Paulina			

(Continued)

	Style	Taste	Sex Appeal
Dina Merrill	_____	_____	_____
. . . Anyone else?			
_____	_____	_____	_____
_____	_____	_____	_____
_____	_____	_____	_____
_____	_____	_____	_____

We laughed for an hour one day, putting this list together. Try to include your friends and make this a "parlor game."

Most of the women we listed are "rich and famous," while most of us are not.

Much has been written about **personality** as the key to **personal style**. But you cannot forget the importance of **lifestyle** when planning a wardrobe. The following Lifestyle Quiz will help you define your clothing needs as they pertain to your lifestyle.

LIFESTYLE QUIZ

1. How much time do you spend in the following situations?
2. What percentage of the money you spend each year on clothes would you allocate to each category?

	% of Time	% of $
Home (leisure or working)	_____	_____
Work (paid or volunteer, out of the home)	_____	_____
Dressy/Formal functions	_____	_____
Sports or Hobbies	_____	_____
Out and About (shopping, errands, just hanging out)	_____	_____

Now, keeping your lifestyle findings in mind, let's move on to **personality**.

Ten women could wear the same outfit, but the one who would stand out the most would be the one with the most imagination and sense of self. It is the ability to dress in your own distinctive, unique way that makes you appear special. Without that understanding, your style can appear dull, imitative, or contrived.

To explore the "real you," complete the following inventory of your inner self:

"WHO AM I"
PERSONALITY INVENTORY

1. How do you see yourself? Circle up to three.
   A. I think of myself as original and artsy.
   B. I think of myself as very feminine and soft.
   C. I think of myself as dramatic.
   D. I think of myself as elegant.
   E. I think of myself as easy-going and casual.
   F. I think of myself as classic and traditional.

2. Which would describe your perfect evening? Circle up to three.

   A. A champagne gallery opening with you in one-of-a-kind clothes.
   B. A summer dance on a romantic terrace with you in organdy.
   C. A theater opening where everyone turns and stares at your high impact outfit.
   D. A fine gourmet dinner for two with you in charmeuse and pearls.
   E. A picnic at an outdoor concert with you in jeans and a sweatshirt.
   F. A dinner and movie with you in updated sportswear.

3. Which skirts do you like the most? Circle up to three.
   A. Handkerchief
   B. Tiered
   C. Sarong
   D. Trumpet
   E. Jean (Denim)
   F. A-Line

4. Which dresses do you like the most? Circle up to three.
   A. Tunic
   B. Strapless
   C. Peplum
   D. Coat Dress
   E. 2-Piece Shirtdress
   F. 1-Piece Shirtdress

5. Which blouses do you like the most? Circle up to three.
   A. Peasant
   B. Ruffle Front
   C. Halter
   D. Surplice

E. Polo
F. Notched Collar

6. Which pants do you like most? Circle up to three.
A. Turkish
B. Palazzo
C. Harem
D. Cropped
E. Jeans
F. Trousers

Count up the total number of circles you have for:
A. _____
B. _____
C. _____
D. _____
E. _____
F. _____

Pick the top three (or less). These are your best style categories. They are:
1. **Artsy**: This style category includes radical chic, individual, costume.
2. **Feminine**: This style category includes romantic, soft, and girlish.
3. **Dramatic**: This category includes high-impact, glitzy, glamorous, and severe.
4. **Elegant**: This category includes monotone, expensive, status, and designer.
5. **Casual**: This category includes denim, separates, coordinates, at-home, and western.
6. **Classic**: This group includes preppy, business, town and country, and all-American.

NOTE: Some women are eclectic. They get up each day and say, "What do I feel like being today?" To do this—to mix all the styles together—takes a massive wardrobe and a real seven-days-a-week love of clothing.

Without pigeonholing or categorizing yourself, let these categories serve as a guideline:

STYLE CATEGORY CHART

	Artsy	Feminine	Dramatic
Colors	Any, but in unusual ways, or monotone with unique accessories or trim	Pastel, soft, or muted, grays	Strong, vivid, and contrasting

(Continued)

STYLE CATEGORY CHART (Continued)

	Artsy	Feminine	Dramatic
Lines	Soft, unconstructed, oversized, layered	Curves, fussiness or simple flow—rounded, never tight	Angular, sharp, asymmetrical, and stylish
Textures	Unusual, silk to sweatshirt to suede	Light, flowing, old-fashioned small prints	Hard, bold, and often overwhelming to a petite
Effect	One-of-a-kind, leader, unique, "far-out"	Fragile, soft, and charming	Confident and chic
Needs	A lifetime collection of unique pieces and a love of putting them together	Gentle, totally womanly clothes—price not an issue	Bold statement clothes and accessories, usually expensive
Favorite Accessory	Pattern shawl, in favorite colors	Lace collar	Bold geometric earrings

	Elegant	Casual	Classic
Colors	Muted and simple tones: earth, gray, black, white, monochrome	Any, but tending to two-color combos: brights, pastels, earth tones	Traditional: beige, navy, red, black
Lines	Uncomplicated, simple, well-fitted, perfect, understated	Unstructured, easy, comfy, and good for motion	Durable, fitted, little, fussy trim
Textures	Fine fabrics, matte or glowing, usually with some motion	Untextured, natural fibers, or blends, flat textures, knits	Natural fibers, small patterns

(Continued)

STYLE CATEGORY CHART (Continued)

	Elegant	Casual	Classic
Effect	Ladylike, refined, cool	Easy-going, athletic, unpretentious, "one-of-the-bunch"	Unoriginal but safe, practical and conservative
Needs	A poised demeanor and clothes that are often major purchases, expensive	Easy pieces, that go together and require easy care	Clothes that will look good year after year, expensive, no wild fashion flings
Favorite Accessory	A real Chanel bag	Canvas, cloth bag	L.L. Bean or Coach bag

Now that we have examined **lifestyle** and **personality** as elements of style, you know what you should to dress your best. Two more elements of style especially important to petites are **proportion** and **scale**.

Let's look at them now.

6

THE ELEMENTS OF STYLE
PROPORTION AND SCALE

Proportion and **Scale** are two words used a great deal in fashion. However, they are intangible in definition, and are not always understood. For a petite, they are especially important words to understand. *Proportion* means the relationship of one thing to another; ideal proportion in fashion balances full with slim, tall with short. *Scale* refers to the size of something in relation to things around it; ideal scale in fashion balances print size or fashion details with the bone and feature scale size of the wearer.

PROPORTION

Thanks to the emergence of the petite market, I can now buy clothes that are "proportion-right" for me. Years ago, I would spend a fortune on alterations and still end up with a garment that was just-off instead of just-right. For an example of proportion, observe the following jacket (Figure 6-1):

A. The jacket

B. The jacket altered, but still wrong

C. The petite jacket—correct in the first place, so why buy anything else?

Figure 6-1 *Alterations can only do so much. Garment "A" is a regular size that needs to be altered to fit a petite customer. Garment "B" is the same jacket with the sleeve shorter and the dart taken in to narrow the body. Jacket "C" is the same style that has been cut for a petite—note the proportion difference.*

To understand clothing proportion, look at the following geometric figures (Figure 6-2).

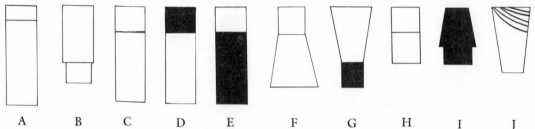

A   B   C   D   E   F   G   H   I   J

Figure 6-2 *Think of the following shapes as representing various outfits. Observe the proportion created by:*

A. An empire tube gown

B. A long, oversized top with a short narrow skirt

C. A blouse and pants of the same color

D. A dark blouse and light pants

E. A light blouse and dark pants

F. A blouse and an A-line skirt

G. A padded shoulder "skimp" top and a narrow skirt

H. A sweater and knee-length skirt of the same color

I. A trapeze top and short skirt

J. An asymmetrically draped, broad-shouldered chemise dress

Proportion is especially important if you have either long or short legs or a short or long waist (Figure 6-3).

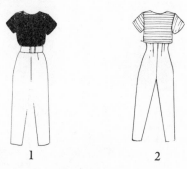

1   2

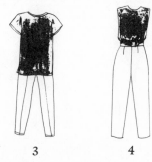

3   4

A. If you are short-waisted, avoid:

1. Belts that match the bottom and contrast with the top

2. High-waisted bottoms and crop tops

If you are short-waisted, choose:

3. Long tops or dropped waists

4. Belts that match the top and contrast with the bottom

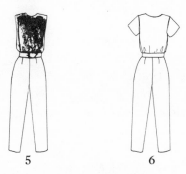

5   6

7   8

If you are long-waisted, avoid:

5. Belts that match the top and contrast with the bottom

6. Tops tucked into bottoms with no belt

Figure 6-3

If you are long-waisted, choose:

7. Overblouses

8. Belts that match the bottom and contrast with the top

Remember that waist and leg length problems are always alleviated by long tops and monotone (one color) dressing.

"I always liked the look of regular size clothes, but I wasn't able to carry them off. Proportioned clothes hit me in the right places, and I don't have to sacrifice style for fit."

—TONY FACCHINI, 5'2.5"

DESIGN PRODUCTION COORDINATOR, ELLEN TRACY

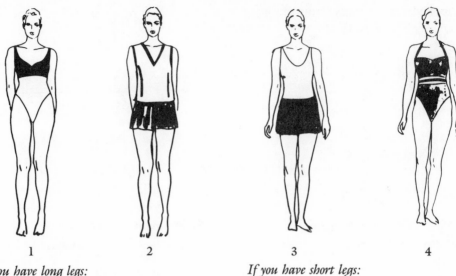

1   2   3   4

B. If you have long legs:

1. Avoid very high cut legs
2. Choose straight cut legs

If you have short legs:

3. Avoid straight cut legs
4. Choose high cut legs

Figure 6-3

PROPORTION TIPS

Here are some important tips for proportional dressing:

For a shorter leg line, wear:

- Full jackets or coats; also, jackets ending at lower hip or mid-thigh.
- Full, pouffy, tiered, ruffled skirts.
- Mini skirts, shorter length skirts, knickers, skorts.
- Detailing such as pant cuffs, thick or bulky textures, and emphasis on light colors.
- Horizontal patterning on skirts, pants, dresses.

To create a slim silhouette for the bottom-heavy figure, wear:

- Details or trimmings at neck and collar, bib collar detail, shoulder width.
- A fitted waistline, no detailing or gathers; instead, try a soft dirndl effect.
- Princess, empire, modified A-line styling.
- Soft draping, "unfussy" styling, or blousing effects.
- Dark colors and patterns for skirts or pants.
- Soft, smooth textures.
- Monotone dressing.

To de-emphasize the top-heavy figure, wear:

- Simple, uncluttered styling for blouses, tops, and jackets. Avoid pockets, neck/collar details, ruffles, pleats, gathers, tucks. Patterns should be small and muted.
- Hip or mid-thigh length jackets, duster coats, long cardigans—avoid breast pockets!
- Simple soft draping, batwing or dolman sleeve effects, dark colors and tones, bloused or tunic tops.

To widen the upper torso, wear:

- Tops and blouses with details such as ruffles, pleats, gathers, pockets, tucks.
- Batwing or dolman sleeves; also, batteau necks, boatnecks, horizontal stripe detailing.
- Light tones or large, bold patterns, etc.

To add emphasis to the lower torso, wear:

- Tunics, tabard vests, dusters, longer length jackets, hip or fanny wraps, peplums, dropped waists, shirring, and gathers add needed dimension.
- Brightness in color and pattern, bulky, stiff or heavy textures, bold patterns, even at the hemline.
- Gathered, full waistline detail, bagginess in contrast to a well-tailored/fitted blouse or top.

Figure 6-4 This long top and knee-length skirt in matching colors, lengthens, slims, and hides any leg or waist proportion problem.

For a longer leg line, wear:

- Lower torso accents and details; look for straight lines or striping, as well as pockets, patchwork or appliqué detail.
- Longer length skirts, cuffless pants.
- Slim line skirts or silhouettes below the hip line.
- Textures that are neither too heavy nor bulky; dark colors (Figure 6-4)!

Equal lengths of tops and bottoms do not always create long, slim proportions but can actually create a cut-up, boxy look (Figure 6-5).

Figure 6-5

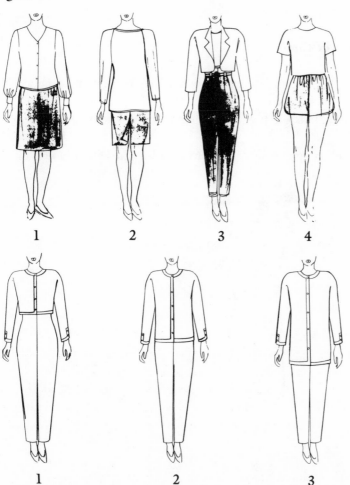

A. The even proportions (1 and 4) tend to look wider and squarish compared to the uneven proportions of long over short or short over long (2 and 3).

B. The same outfit in different proportions—the changes in proportion have less effect on the overall look, as the outfits are monotone from head to toe —very elongating and slimming.

Equal and unequal lengths in tops and bottoms create very different illusions of height and width, as do variable hem lengths.

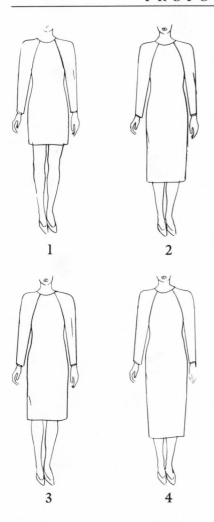

1   2

3   4

C. Many hem lengths can be attractive, but (1) is so short that it will make most women look wider; (2) is a graceful length, but it ends at the widest part of the calf, which tends to make the legs look heavy; (3), which ends just below the knee, and (4), which ends well below the widest part of the calf, are the best bets for most women.

SCALE

Scale is perhaps the least understood fashion term. It refers to the **size** of a print, check, floral, plaid, or stripe **as it relates to the particular wearer**.

Many women think that scale is in proportion to height or to dress size. However, scale is based on and is a reflection of your overall configuration, which is made up of:

- Bone structure
- Facial feature size
- General build (do people see you as delicate, average, strong, etc.?)

To determine scale, hold fabric samples up to your face, and see which size print looks best on you. Invite a friend to help. Print samples of different sizes can be hard to find, so try your scale test with our paper samples (Figure 6-6).

Figure 6-6 *Which dot or stripe looks best on you?*

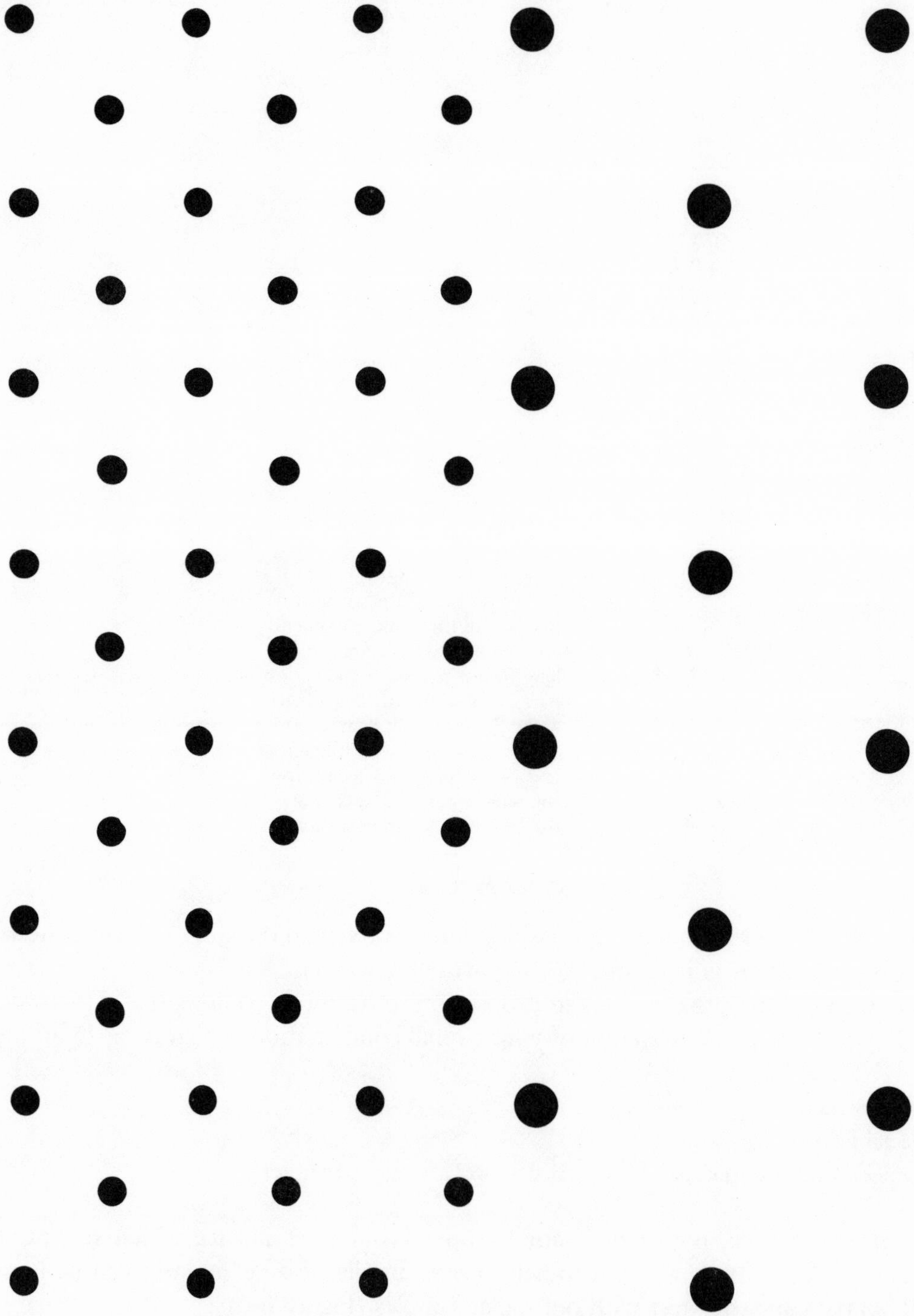

Figure 6-6 *(Continued)*

Figure 6-6 *(Continued)*

Figure 6-6 (Continued)

	DOT	STRIPE
1. Small	_____	_____
2. Medium-Small	_____	_____
3. Medium	_____	_____
4. Large	_____	_____

What is your best scale? _____

Figure 6-7

A. The difference scales of these two plaids make a big difference in the overall look of each dress.

Remember, scale is not always a matter of height and size alone, but a combination of many elements. A large woman is not necessarily large in **scale**, nor a small woman necessarily small in scale.

Medium- and large-scale designs have much more impact on the overall look of a garment than do small designs (Figure 6-7).

Figure 6-7

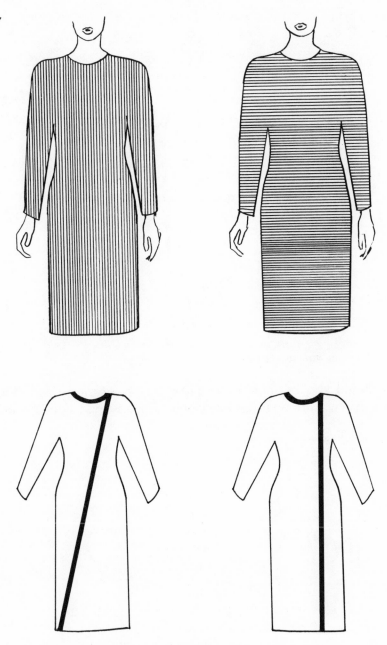

B. Small-scale patterns do not affect the look of a garment as much as larger scale prints or garments with very bold lines.

1. These two dresses are little changed by the direction of the small-scale stripe

2. These two dresses are more dramatically different due to the boldness of the trim

Figure 6-8 *What's wrong with this picture?*

Accessories should also be in scale with the person wearing them (Figure 6-8). Sometimes, you may want to wear just one emphatic accessory. Rhonda Spurlock, 5′1″,

Figure 6-9 *See how the emphasis moves to the:*

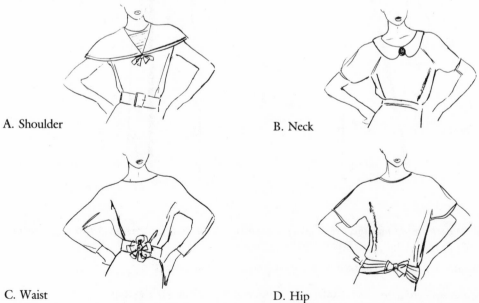

A. Shoulder

B. Neck

C. Waist

D. Hip

the fashion director for Dillard's in San Antonio, is one of the best-dressed women I know. She likes to wear one color from head to toe, with a major piece of jewelry— near her face.

But remember, scale must be considered here also, lest the accessory wear you! Your face should dominate your look to draw the eye upward, building height. Never emphasize any part of your figure you wish to play down, *e.g.*, no big, flashy pins on large breasts, etc. (Figure 6-9).

SUMMARY: ELEMENTS OF STYLE PERSONAL "EXAM"

Now that you are on your way to becoming a fashion expert, you are ready for a "pop" quiz!

1. Name the colors that you know to be your best (up to 12 colors):

_____ _____ _____

_____ _____ _____

_____ _____ _____

_____ _____ _____

2. What is your body type: _____

3. What textures do you like best: _____

_____

4. Which silhouette types are best for your figure:

Dresses: _____

_____

Tops: _____

_____

Bottoms: _____

_____

Coats/Jackets: _____

_____

Lingerie: _____

_____

Bathing Suits: _____

_____

5. What are your most flattering figure traits: _____

_____

_____

6. What are your least flattering figure traits: _____

_____

_____

7. What are your best (or favorite) styles (list no more than three):
   1. _____
   2. _____
   3. _____

8. What is your overall body scale: _____

_____

What do you want to emphasize on your figure: _____

_____

_____

What do you want to de-emphasize on your figure: _____

_____

_____

Describe your lifestyle: _____

_____

_____

9. Do you have any proportion problems: _____
   Legs   _____
   Waist   _____

Others _____

If you have been able to fill in this quiz readily, then you have taken a great deal of time to work the preceding chapters. Congratulations! Your time and effort have been rewarded with the very information that some women pay hundreds of dollars to get from professional image consultants.

Now, on to the clothes themselves!

7

EVERYTHING YOU EVER WANTED TO KNOW ABOUT CLOTHES

THE ADVANTAGES OF PETITE SIZES

The petite fashion industry has redesigned clothing, changing proportion and fit to give us advantages that misses sizes can't. You should learn to spot these advantages, so that you will be able to pick the clothes that are best for you, and need the fewest (if any) alterations. Here are some of the details that make petite clothes fit better.

1. Shoulder seams are aligned directly on the shoulder and do not slip or shift back and forth.

2. Shoulder pads (if any) are proportioned for petites—flatter, smaller, and contoured for a smaller shoulder. You won't get that "House of Pancakes" look when wearing multiple layers of clothes with shoulder pads.

3. Armholes are raised, reshaped, and scaled down for proportion, fit, and comfort. Sleeveless armholes won't show more skin or lingerie than you would like, either.

4. Bottoms (skirts and pants) are narrower, shorter, more shaped, and less bulky.

5. The "sweep" or bottom edge of skirts, blouses, or dresses are about the same width as the same size in misses sizes, giving comfort in hip room or stride.

6. Waistbands are re-proportioned to the compactness of the petite torso. Waist treatments and waistbands are shorter and trimmer.

7. Darts begin and end where they should and are shorter.

8. Details such as belts, buttons, zippers, flanges, pleats, plackets, ruffles, embroidery, embellishment, and appliqué have been scaled down in size, depth, and quantity. You can wear them without looking fussy, frowsy, or overwhelmed.

9. Collars fit without gaping, riding up, grazing your jawline, or hitting you in the ear! Petite necklines are re-proportioned in drop and depth to lie flatter on us; collars are scaled down and reduced in their "spread," and jabots, lace collars, and ruffles are slightly smaller.

10. Volume of fabric, pleats, shirring, and gathers are minimized.

11. Pockets are shorter in placement and smaller in size, depth, flap, and trim size.

12. Full or even billowing sleeves and wide or loose cuffs are reduced so they are not overwhelming on the petite.

13. Patterns, repeats, and decorative motifs are reduced anywhere from 5% to 20%, depending on the size of the pattern.

14. Petite dresses in sheer fabrics, such as voile or georgette, are sold with underslips that fit well and have shortened straps that won't fall down.

15. Strapless dresses, whether for day or evening, won't sag or buckle.

Once you have learned how to measure yourself and recognize the elements of your own personal style, the next step in becoming *The Complete Petite* is to become knowledgeable about clothing—**the clothing that is right for you**! The following style charts are designed to give you general knowledge of clothing and to allow you to recognize the styles that specifically flatter your figure—and to build a workable wardrobe to satisfy your lifestyle.

Here are **style charts**, arranged by category, preceded by special **tips**.

DRESSES

Dresses are best-sellers in Petite Departments, and they are my personal favorites, too. Easy to wear, appropriate for almost any occasion, a dress eliminates the need for mixing several pieces of clothing.

I've had some of my dresses for years—part of the benefit of not growing any taller since the ninth grade!

The following **tips** will help you build a great collection of dresses:

1. Always buy the best **quality** that you can afford. Inferior quality dresses can break down in fabric or workmanship under normal wear and tear. (*See* Shopping Tips in Chapter 10.)

2. If you are going to wear a dress that is **strapless, mini, or extreme** in any way, make sure you have the poise and confidence to carry it off—nothing looks worse than a woman tugging at the top or bottom of her dress because she is self-conscious in it.

3. Just covering the **knees** makes legs look longer. Hubert Givenchy says that a woman's knees are the ugliest part of her body—like elbows, they show age quickly.

4. **Vertical stripes, trims, and ornamentations**, from the neckline to the hem, give a long, lean line to the body. Horizontal details look better at the neckline or at the waist, rather than at the hem.

5. **Details**, from the size of prints, to peplums, ruffles, trims, buttons, and pleats, should all be in proportion to the size of the dress and of the person wearing it.

6. **Daytime dresses** should have simple necklines, a natural shoulder line, ample room in the skirt for walking comfortably, and simple, short, ¾, or long sleeves (sleeveless only if you have great upper arms). The best colors for daytime dresses are those that blend easily with your accessories, coats, and jackets. Such colors are black, beige, camel, navy, gray, wine, dark green, red, royal blue, soft blue, white, ecru, and soft pastels. The best fabrics are natural fibers such as cotton, wool, linen, silk, and synthetics or blends such as polyester or poly/cotton, poly/wool, or rayon. (*See* Fabrics in Chapter 10.)

7. **Evening dresses** in dressy fabrics create a more festive or after-five feeling. Good evening fabrics are lace, velvet, silk, taffeta, satin, peau de soie, jersey, wool, cotton, linen, and rayon. Evening clothes can be any color, although the all-time favorite seems to be black. Black, however does not look well on all women, and must be worn with clearly defined makeup colors, such as red or hot pink for lips and cheeks, and smokey tones for eyes. In general, many women make the mistake of wearing little or no make-up with evening clothes, and looking washed out in the evening when artificial light tends to drain color. If you do not wear makeup because you fear looking painted, or if you

think there is even a tiny chance that your makeup looks outdated, seek either professional advice or the advice of a friend who is good with her makeup.

The following illustrations give examples of dresses without emphasis at the waist (Figure 7-1), dresses with a high or low waist (Figure 7-2), and dresses with emphasis at the waist (Figure 7-3).

Figure 7-1 Dresses without emphasis at the waist.

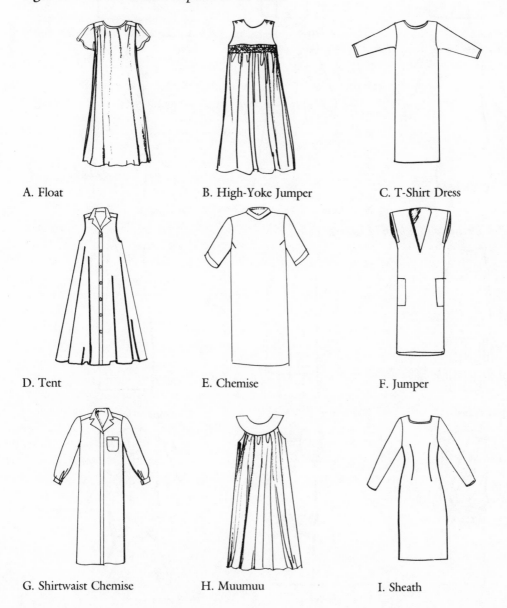

A. Float

B. High-Yoke Jumper

C. T-Shirt Dress

D. Tent

E. Chemise

F. Jumper

G. Shirtwaist Chemise

H. Muumuu

I. Sheath

Figure 7-1 (Continued)

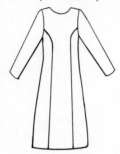

J. Princess

K. Coat Dress

L. Slip Dress

M. Sweater

N. A-Line

O. Tabard

Figure 7-2 Dresses with a high or low waist.

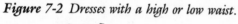

A. Dropped Waist

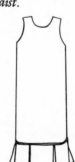

B. Flapper

C. Empire

D. Fanny Wrap

E. Thigh Wrap

F. Tie Front

Figure 7-2 *(Continued)*

G. V-Yoke

H. Baby Doll

I. Peasant

J. 2-Piece Blouson

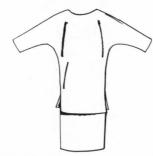

K. Tunic Dress

L. 2-Piece Overblouse

M. Dropped Waist (Elastic)

N. Dropped Waist (Hip)

Figure 7-3 *Dresses with emphasis at the waist.*

A. Set-in Waist Sheath

B. Set-in Waist Dirndl

C. 1-Piece Shirtdress

Figure 7-3 *(Continued)*

D. Elastic Waist

E. Surplice

F. Wrap

G. 2-Piece Shirtdress

H. Cinch

I. Peplum

J. Pinafore

K. Schoolgirl Blouson

L. Prairie

M. Sundress

N. Strapless

O. Longuette/Bustier

P. Peasant

PANTS

My mom's #1 rule for buying pants is simply to turn around, look in the rear view mirror, and take an objective look!

Most women can find pants that will flatter their particular size and figure, but who among us has not seen that disaster-on-wheels wearing a pair of pants that gives a horrifying, unflattering, backward view?

Here is a simple way to determine which pants are best for you. Examine your waist and hip area to see which areas are biggest and need to be de-emphasized. Choose pants loosest in those areas; an exaggerated example of this would be jodhpurs on a woman who has heavy thighs—they won't know if you or the pants are full. Similarly, women with large waists and small thighs might choose elastic-waist leggings to show off trim legs and yet fit comfortably around a problematic mid-section.

Here are some more **tips** on pants:

1. **Trousers** are pants that are tailored, usually with pleats in the front. They are almost always made of a medium-weight fabric that drapes well, such as blends, cotton, wool crepe, or light weight corduroy. Pleat-front pants are very flattering on women who are either very thin, or who have a tummy bulge.
2. **Jeans** are usually made of denim, although I have seen them in rayon, twill and silk. Since they are meant to fit snugly, take care to choose jeans that fit correctly, flatter good points, and minimize problem areas. If you choose "paper bag" waistbands or baggy style jeans, be sure to look for proportions that flatter, to avoid looking dumpy or short-waisted.
3. **Pantsuits** are perennial favorites for day and evening wear.

The following style charts group pants by those that tend to be narrow (Figure 7-4), and those that tend to be full (Figure 7-5).

Figure 7-4 Pants that tend to be narrow.

A. Straight Leg   B. Peg Leg   C. Stirrup

Figure 7-4 *(Continued)*

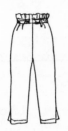

D. Cropped

E. Legging

F. Capri

G. Knicker

H. Toreador

I. Pedal Pusher

Figure 7-5 *Pants that tend to be full.*

A. Pleated Trousers

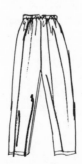

B. Pajama

C. Sweats

D. Short Sport Culotte

E. Gathered Culotte

F. Cuffed Culotte

Figure 7-5 *(Continued)*

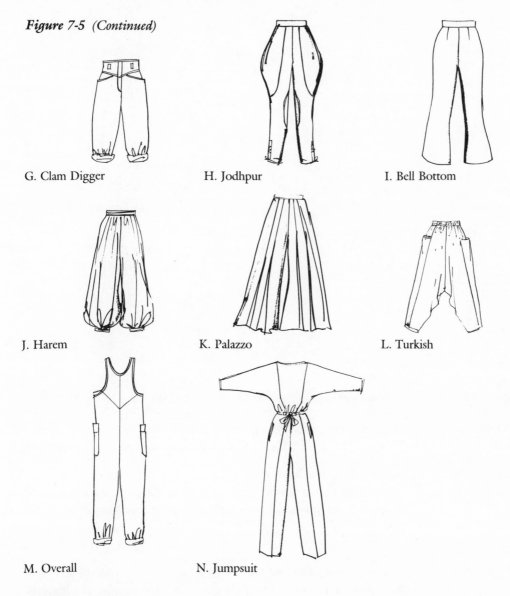

G. Clam Digger   H. Jodhpur   I. Bell Bottom

J. Harem   K. Palazzo   L. Turkish

M. Overall   N. Jumpsuit

A Note on Jeans

Denim jeans (Figure 7-6) have been worn by miners in the Gold Rush of 1849, cowboys, bobby soxers in the 1940s, and flower children of the late Sixties. Today, they are worn by every segment of society, and the design and selection have never been better. Every jean doesn't look great on every body, so here's an easy guide to finding a jean that's best for your body type.

PROBLEM: Long-waisted (Long torso, short leg)
SOLUTION: Always wear high-waist jeans with a plain belt.

Figure 7-6 Jeans.

 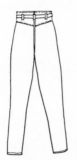  

A. High Waist   B. No Back Pocket   C. Snug, Tapered   D. Straight Leg

E. Contour Waistband   F. Spandex Cotton   G. High "Paper Bag" Waist   H. Slash Pocket

PROBLEM: Short-waisted (Short torso, long leg)
SOLUTION: Pick low-rise jeans with a belt that matches the top of your outfit.

PROBLEM: Saddlebags (Low hip bumps)
SOLUTION: Avoid snug fit, opt for straight legs instead. Contour waistbands and dropped front yokes with soft gathers disguise saddlebags. Try elastic waists.

PROBLEM: Protruding stomach
SOLUTION: Spandex cotton jeans are the newest look, and offer control and comfort. Avoid side and back zippers, go for fly front zippers, not buttons.

PROBLEM: Short legs
SOLUTION: Create a longer line by wearing high waists, full length legs and tapered legs. Avoid short, cuffed styles

PROBLEM: Fat ankles
SOLUTION: Buy wider, longer styles.

PROBLEM: Thin ankles
SOLUTION: Cropped, capri, ankle zips are best.

PROBLEM: Large derriere

SOLUTION: Avoid large back pockets with fancy detail. Wear dark blue new denim, not stone- or acid-washes.

PROBLEM: Small derriere (flat)

SOLUTION: Snug, tapered styles with contour stitching to add interest. "Distressed denim" is a good fabric choice over stiff, new denim. Patterns, chintzes, checks and light, shiny materials are fine.

PROBLEM: Heavy thighs

SOLUTION: Avoid tapered legs that minimize calf and draw attention to upper leg. Natural dark blue denims are best.

PROBLEM: Thin thighs

SOLUTION: Appliqués, baggy front pockets, florals, paisleys and bold striping look great. Deep front pleats, ornamental seams give drape and shape.

PROBLEM: Thick waist

SOLUTION: Buy sewn-in waistbands, and only wear thin or medium width belts. Avoid pleated waistbands.

SHORTS

Shorts (Figures 7-7 and 7-8) of any kind will only look good if they "cut" your leg in the most flattering place possible, which means wherever it is *not overly wide*. Short shorts should only be worn by those with good legs, and Bermuda shorts may only be worn by those with shapely legs. The rest of us will find a fuller pleated front or gathered elastic-waist short with longer length and more fullness in the leg the best look.

Figure 7-7 Shorts.

A. Short-Shorts

B. Shorts

C. Wide Leg Cuffed

D. Tap Pants

E. Boxer

F. Skort (a combination skirt/short)

G. Pleated

H. Jamaica

Figure 7-7 *(Continued)*

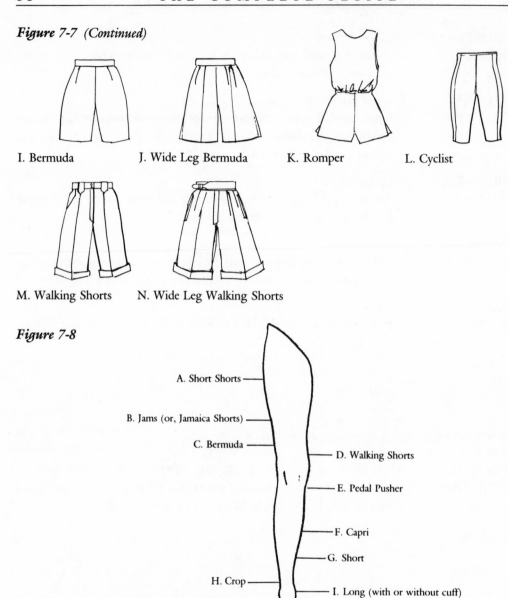

I. Bermuda   J. Wide Leg Bermuda   K. Romper   L. Cyclist

M. Walking Shorts   N. Wide Leg Walking Shorts

Figure 7-8

A. Short Shorts
B. Jams (or, Jamaica Shorts)
C. Bermuda
D. Walking Shorts
E. Pedal Pusher
F. Capri
G. Short
H. Crop
I. Long (with or without cuff)

Some common lengths for shorts and pants.

SKIRTS

Skirts are a major part of any woman's wardrobe. Clearly the most feminine and traditional of separates, skirts can be great wardrobe extenders and very flattering "bottoms."

Some rules to obey:

- If your legs are particularly short or heavy, **don't** wear mini or micro skirts.
- **Don't** imagine that misses short skirts are ideal for the petite woman—only petite short skirts have the correct proportions.

Skirts are often referred to by inch lengths, so it helps to know the following (Figure 7-9).

Figure 7-9

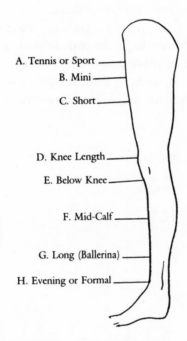

A. Tennis or Sport

B. Mini

C. Short

D. Knee Length

E. Below Knee

F. Mid-Calf

G. Long (Ballerina)

H. Evening or Formal

Visual illustrations of some common skirt (or dress) lengths.

These measurements may have a different meaning for petites, as the following chart explains.

Skirt Lengths (Based on an average height of 5′4″)

This chart is a simple one to help you understand skirt lengths when they are described in inches.

18 inches	Reaches mid-thigh
22 inches	Reaches top of the knee
25 inches	Falls 2 inches below the knee

(Continued)

27 inches	Calf length
32 inches	Falls below calf, above ankle

Culottes and Gaucho Skirts

Culottes are making a comeback, but make sure they are of a flattering cut. Culottes are devastatingly horrible on bottom-heavy women, or anyone with bowed legs.

Whether a skirt is made of silk or grass, it should drape in a way that will enhance your bottom area, and should allow freedom of movement. Pleat treatments can look extremely feminine as they move gracefully with you as you walk or sit. Novelty skirts—poufs, minis, tiered, flounced, Spanish, and balloon skirts—all come and go and return again! Remember to buy **petite** skirts in these styles, as modifying or altering misses skirts to new lengths will often throw off the proportions (Figures 7-10 and 7-11).

Figure 7-10 Skirts that tend to be narrow in form.

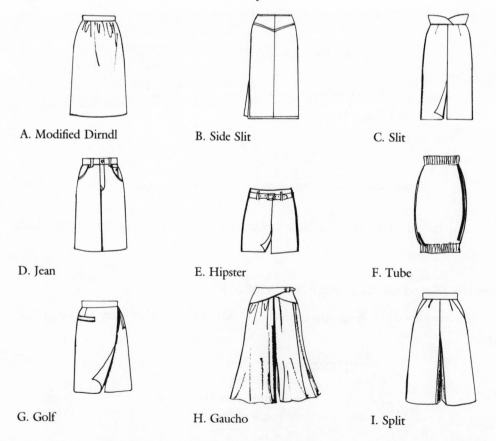

A. Modified Dirndl   B. Side Slit   C. Slit

D. Jean   E. Hipster   F. Tube

G. Golf   H. Gaucho   I. Split

Figure 7-10 (Continued)

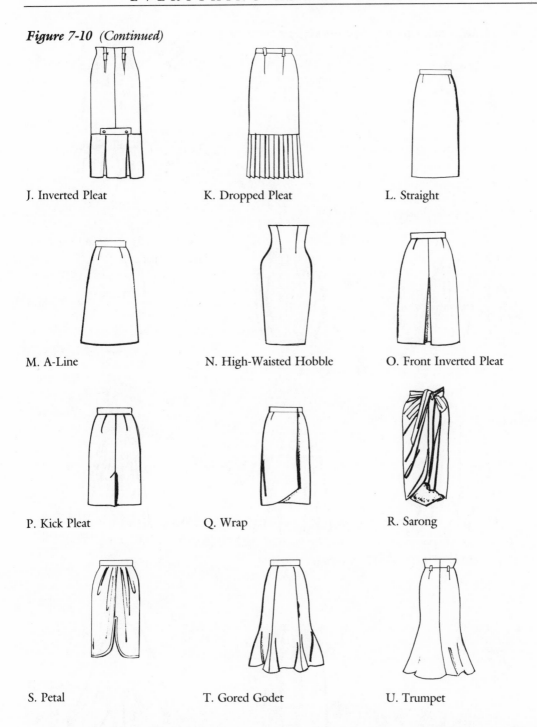

J. Inverted Pleat

K. Dropped Pleat

L. Straight

M. A-Line

N. High-Waisted Hobble

O. Front Inverted Pleat

P. Kick Pleat

Q. Wrap

R. Sarong

S. Petal

T. Gored Godet

U. Trumpet

Remember, that skirt width can affect the overall size appearance of the wearer (Figure 7-12).

Figure 7-11 *Skirts that tend to be full in form.*

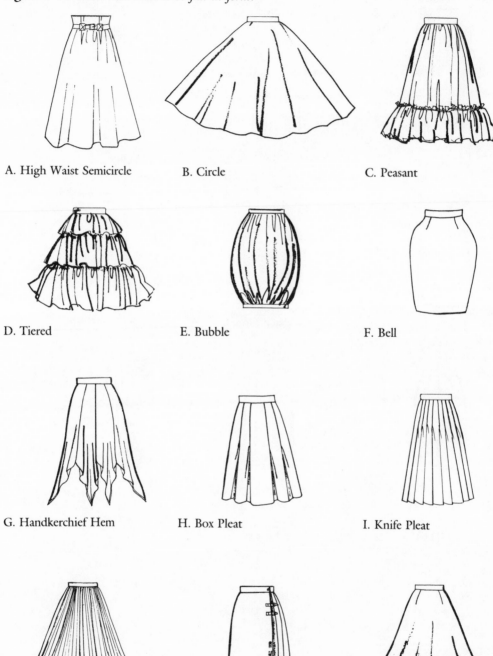

A. High Waist Semicircle

B. Circle

C. Peasant

D. Tiered

E. Bubble

F. Bell

G. Handkerchief Hem

H. Box Pleat

I. Knife Pleat

J. Crystal Pleat

K. Kilt

L. Flared Semicircle

Figure 7-11 *(Continued)*

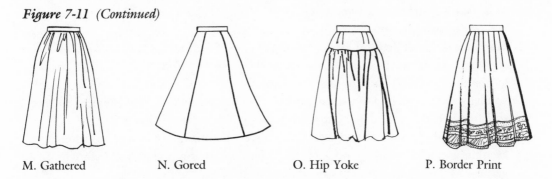

M. Gathered   N. Gored   O. Hip Yoke   P. Border Print

Figure 7-12 *The width of a skirt can affect the visual width and height of the wearer. The first three skirts are too wide and full, and will make the wearer appear larger and shorter than she is. The second threesome are more slimming, height-engendering, and flattering.*

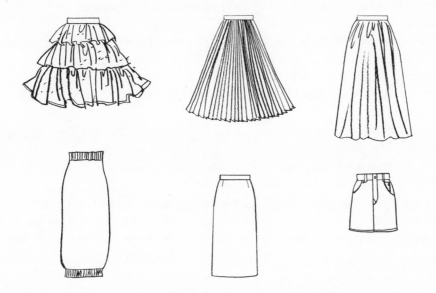

TOPS: BLOUSES, SHIRTS, AND
SWEATERS

Blouses and shirts are the backbone of your wardrobe. They can update a suit, revamp skirts and pants, enhance separates, and give casual wear and jeans a fresh look.

Quality transcends designer labels and high prices. Less expensive clothes can fit and wear as well as the pricey ones. Here's how to spot good quality in a top (Figures 7-13 and 7-14):

1. **Fabric** should feel pleasant to the touch. Rub it between your fingers, or slip a hand inside the garment. Does it feel irritating? If it is a synthetic, does it feel soft and natural,

or is there a clammy, overly warm sensation? A quick touch test can tell how the blouse will feel against your body after hours of wearing.

2. Test for **wrinkle-ability**. Squeeze a handful of fabric for about ten seconds, then release, and watch the fabric reaction. Do the creases begin to relax and smooth out, or do they look as though they'll need ironing? After normal wear, clothes shouldn't look as though you have slept in them. Only linen, organdy, organza, taffeta, and the like need to have stiffeners added to stay crisp. Other fabrics should drape smoothly.

3. Check the **fabric content and care label** to see what maintenance will be required to keep the garment looking good. Consider your time, energy and budget before buying garments that require constant dry cleaning or delicate, hand care.

4. Never buy a blouse or shirt (or any other garment) that is **too tight**. Not only is an item that pulls or gapes unflattering, but the fabric will stretch or break down. Wearing a garment that is too tight is giving a guided tour of every lump and bump in your figure—you will need a perfect shape to pull it off, and even then, you will still look cheap.

5. Check the **workmanship**. Seams should not pucker or show loose stitching; plaids and patterns should match; all trims should be firmly attached; and finally, fusings and interfacings should not appear thick or shiny.

6. Check the **color of the fabric** for discoloration from faulty dye lots, fading from lights, or spots or stains.

7. If the top is **knit, and on a hanger**, check for stretching, or "growing" of the garment. Also, check the ribbing around the bottom or cuffs for elasticity.

8. Check the **closeness of the weave** if you are concerned with durability. Loose weaves tend to be better for clothes worn occasionally.

9. **Knits** often run small due to shrinkage in steam pressing, and sometimes you may need to wear a size or several sizes larger than usual. Don't let the size number bother you, and bear in mind that nothing is more "fattening" than a sweater that is too tight.

Figure 7-13 Blouses and shirts.

A. Side Slit Camp Shirt   B. Man's Style Shirt   C. Dolman Sleeve Scoop Neck T-Shirt

D. Mock Turtle, Dolman Sleeves   E. Peasant Blouse   F. Bishop Blouse

Figure 7-13 (Continued)

G. 3/4 Sleeve Stock Tie Blouse

H. Cassock

I. Kimono Blouse

J. Draped Cowl

K. Jabot

L. Surplice

M. Hip Yoked Surplice

N. Notched Collar

O. Double Breasted Notch

P. Raglan High Collar

Q. High Collared Painter's Shirt

R. Raglan Bow Blouse

S. Deep V-Neck Bow Blouse

T. Camisole

U. Muscle Top

V. V-Neck T-Shirt

W. Tank Top

X. Crew Neck
T-Shirt

Y. Boat Neck Cap
Sleeve T-Shirt

Z. Shell

Figure 7-13 *(Continued)*

AA. Square Neck Drop-Shoulder Blouse

BB. Surplice

CC. Ruffled Front

DD. Cossack

EE. Blouson

FF. Collarless Button Front

GG. Sailor

HH. Fanny Wrap

II. Collar Band

JJ. Polo

KK. Halter

Figure 7-14 *Sweaters and vests.*

A. Crew

B. Cardigan

C. V-Neck

D. V-Necked Cardigan

E. Fisherman's

F. Turtleneck

Figure 7-14 (Continued)

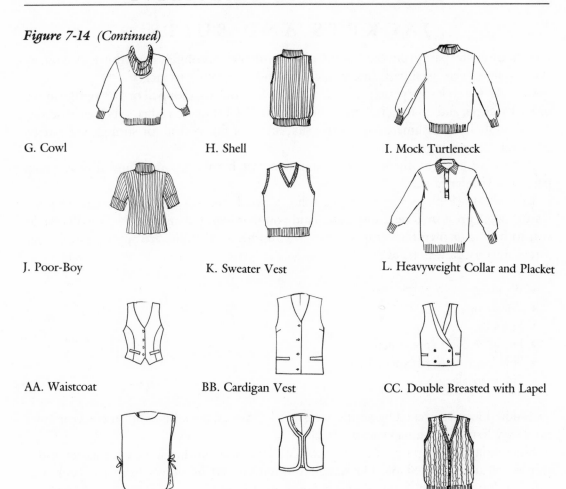

G. Cowl　　　　　　H. Shell　　　　　　I. Mock Turtleneck

J. Poor-Boy　　　　K. Sweater Vest　　　L. Heavyweight Collar and Placket

AA. Waistcoat　　　BB. Cardigan Vest　　CC. Double Breasted with Lapel

DD. Tabard　　　　　EE. Bolero Vest　　　FF. Sweater Vest

The following shows where sleeves should and will end, if you buy petite sizes (Figure 7-15).

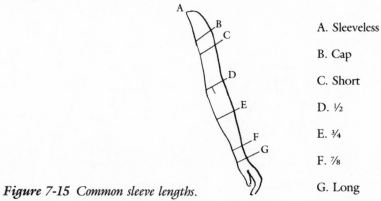

A. Sleeveless

B. Cap

C. Short

D. ½

E. ¾

F. ⅞

G. Long

Figure 7-15 Common sleeve lengths.

JACKETS AND SUITS

Jackets are a vital part of anyone's wardrobe, going with absolutely everything. A woman can get along very well with one single skirt and four fabulous jackets.

Great jacket styles for petites include Eisenhower, bolero, cropped or ¾ length, riding or hack jackets, and evening jackets, plain or quilted. Choose rich fabrics such as brocade, tweed, mohair, or cashmere for winter; silk, linen, or fine cotton for spring; and taffeta or velvet for evening.

Jackets are great by themselves, to mix and match with separates and dresses or as part of a wonderful suit.

Like a blue chip stock in your portfolio, a good suit is a solid investment in your wardrobe. A great interview suit could land you that high-paying job, which will enable you to buy your own blue chip stocks (and another suit). Suits are appropriate for all forays into social waters, especially:

- Weddings
- Christenings
- Funerals
- Dramatic court appearances
- Ship launchings, ribbon cuttings
- Public speaking

Tailored looks softened by gentle accessories (scarves, pins, bows) or menswear suits on a very feminine woman can be dazzling.

Suits today are shaplier and more vibrant. The ideal suit has a well-cut jacket and a slim or pleated skirt. Skirts, like hats, are often viewed by others from the back and sides, so look carefully from all angles before you buy.

Petite suits are completely scaled down, so that shoulder pads, collars, lapels, pockets, jacket lengths, and skirt treatments look and feel just right (Figure 7-16).

Figure 7-16 Jackets.

A. Blazer   B. Double Breasted   C. Collarless/Boxy Cut

Figure 7-16 (Continued)

D. Pea Coat

E. Tuxedo

F. Semi-Fitted

G. Chanel Type

H. Peplum

I. Bolero

J. Eton

K. Spencer

L. Norfolk

M. Safari

N. Eisenhower

O. Nehru

P. Mandarin

Q. Unstructured

R. Wingback Jacket

Figure 7-16 (Continued)

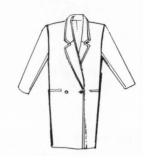

S. Trapeze or Fly-Away   T. ¾ Topper   U. Car Coat

V. Stroller   W. Parka

COATS

For the best outerwear looks, keep the following in mind:

1. Tight weaves make the warmest coats. Go for poplin, gabardine, nylon, and taffeta.
2. Best basic coat colors are khaki, gray, olive, or black. Best second coats are in bright solids and jewel tones (blue, red, teal, purple), and patterns (checks, plaids, and tweeds).
3. Petite fur coats have less bulk than regular sizes.
4. Check labels on raincoats and trenchcoats. "Waterproof" means the coat is plastic or rubber coated, and impervious to water. "Water Repellent" is a "Scotchguard" or silicone-treated fabric like "Zepel." "Permanent" finishes don't need to be reapplied, and "temporary" finishes must be reapplied. Let your dry cleaner do it for best results.

Petite women have two major gripes when buying petite coats:

- The color range is limited. Older women don't want dull colors or salt and pepper tweeds, and younger customers want vibrant colors and newer styles.
- Lengths are often still too **long**, even though the body of the coat may fit beautifully. Sleeves can be too big in width.

On the bright side, however, petites now have real and fake fur coats available. You've got to try them on to see what a difference in proportion and comfort there is! A good coat is a major purchase. Here are some helpful hints for choosing one (Figures 7-17 and 7-18):

Figure 7-17 *Narrow coats.*

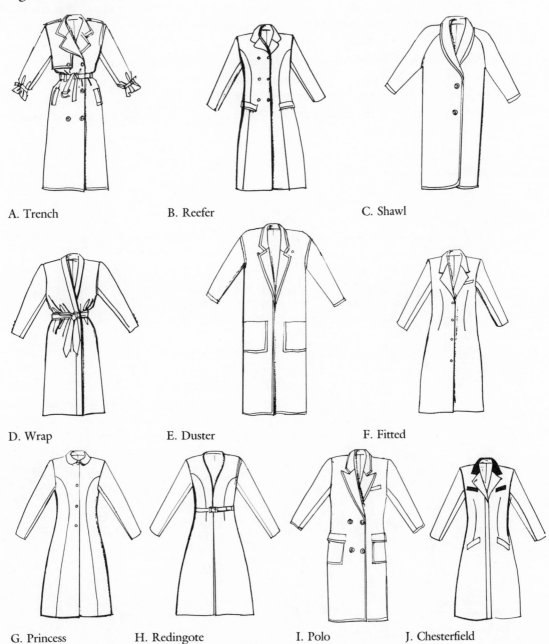

A. Trench   B. Reefer   C. Shawl

D. Wrap   E. Duster   F. Fitted

G. Princess   H. Redingote   I. Polo   J. Chesterfield

1. Pick a full length coat that can be worn for daytime and evening.
2. Make sure the coat color goes with the majority of clothes in your wardrobe.
3. Never buy a coat that's too small or too tight.
4. Three-quarter length coats can go to the office and out for the weekend over casual wear. Brighter, bolder colors like royal blue, yellow, fuschia, or kelly green are terrific.
5. Everyone should own a trench coat, in beige, olive green, navy, or black. If it has a removable lining, so much the better. (Rex Harrison once said the English often wear their wool liners as bathrobes!)
6. Raincoats can be wool- or fur-lined for fall and winter. For rainy spring days, there are great new vinyls in checks, brights, and embossed patterns available now. They're easy to roll up and stash when the sun comes out again.
7. Canvas and denim "dusters" are now made in petite sizes—they look wonderful with easy trousers or jeans.

Figure 7-18 *Full coats.*

A. Swagger   B. Cape   C. Sherlock Holmes Cape

D. Balmacaan   E. Smock   F. Fling   G. Quilted

The following shows where jackets and coats should and will end, if you buy petite sizes (Figure 7–19).

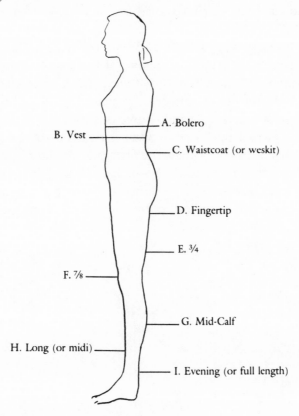

Figure 7-19 Here are the common jacket and coat lengths.

LINGERIE

Pretty lingerie is making a comeback with the return of ultra-feminine clothes, but it's been a long time coming for petites.

Several years ago, I gave a fashion show for a major department store, and brought out two nightgowns and two slips (one full slip, one half slip) newly available in petite sizes. I showed the differences in proportion between regular misses and petites, and introduced the store's lingerie fitter who explained that she would be available to meet interested customers and schedule appointments for them after the show. She might well have said that there was a million dollars in cold cash waiting for them as well—it was all I could do to keep them in their seats throughout the show; luckily, some minor mishaps held their attention (a broken microphone, falling decorations, a half-dressed model), until the stampede to the lingerie fitter. These women were long overdue for undergarments that were well-designed, comfortable, and elegant.

There is no need to put up with hanging slips, straps that slide, nightgowns that drag, and bathrobes that act like dust mops. Today, there are teddies, tap pants, body suits, camisoles, and garter belts, all designed for the body-conscious petite (Figures 7-20, 7-21, and 7-22).

In my work as a fitting model, I find a body suit convenient. At other times, I prefer briefs or high rise panties as they don't show VLPs (*Visible Panty Lines*). I also go through a lot of pantyhose. I have found that inexpensive hosiery tends to run short in the leg, so I'll buy a medium size if I'm economizing. Expensive hose has its plus side: it wears better and has a better tone and degree of sheerness.

No matter what hosiery I buy, I never wear it right out of the package—I wash it first. This removes chemicals and softens the fiber, and the hose don't seem to "run" as fast. Always wash hose after every wearing—it lasts far longer.

Mom always told me to wear clean underwear in case I was in an accident and had to go to the hospital, where the medical staff would see me. I can see the medical report:

Figure 7-20 Lingerie for at home and sleepwear.

A. Bathrobe   B. Kimono   C. Hostess Coat

D. Caftan   E. Housecoat   F. Robe

Figure 7-20 *(Continued)*

G. Baby Doll

H. Big T-Shirt

I. Peignoir and Negligee

J. Illusion Caftan

K. Short Nightgown

L. Nightshirt

M. Shorty Pajamas

N. Empire Gown

O. Pajamas

P. Granny Gown

". . . fractured collarbone, terminal bra strap . . ." However, you will find that your fine undergarments last longer if you launder them **by hand**, or use a net/mesh bag in the washing machine. Air dry them so that they retain their elasticity and shape. Padded bras and underwires particularly break down quickly in the dryer.

With all of the stress and hassle that women go through all day long, it's comforting to know that you're wearing fabulous lacy little nothings under your conservative suit or your sweatshirt and jeans.

Figure 7-21 Foundations.

A. Body Briefer   B. Corselette   C. Merry Widow

D. Soft Cup Bra   E. Underwire Bra   F. Capri Girdle

G. Waist Cincher   H. Control Brief   I. Panty Girdle   J. Thigh Panty Girdle

K. Strapless Bra   L. Longline Bra   M. Bustier

Figure 7-21 (Continued)

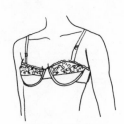
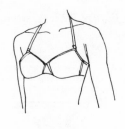

N. Contour Bra   O. Sport Bra   P. Push-Up or Demi Bra   Q. Convertible Bra

Figure 7-22 Daywear.

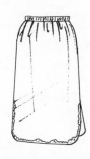

A. Full Slip   B. Half Slip   C. Petticoat or Crinoline

D. Split Petticoat   E. Bare Camisole   F. Bikini

G. Fuller Camisole   H. Brief   I. Teddy

Figure 7-22 (Continued)

J. High-Cut Panty   K. Tap Pant   L. T-Shirt   M. Body Suit
                                                               (with Shoulder Pads)

LINGERIE/UNDERWEAR

Expensive	Moderate	Sport/Thermal
Silks	Nylon	Wool Flannel
Satins	Orlon	Silk
Cashmeres	Dacron	Cotton
Fine Cottons	Cotton/Poly Blends	Cotton/Poly Blends
Lace Trim		
Good Flannels		

BATHING SUITS

Bathing suits are made of Lycra, nylon or elasticized cotton and are self-adjusting to the body. There are a few rules for buying bathing suits that particularly apply to petites (Figure 7-23):

1. Never shop for a suit when you're depressed and overweight. Those hideous fluorescent lights and the three-way mirrors in the dressing room are enough to make the strongest woman weep, and the slimmest woman suicidal. Don't bring the salesperson or your mother into the fitting room with you, although a sister or close friend (if they're not too catty) is okay. You can commiserate in agony together, and have brunch afterwards (since you'll diet tomorrow anyway).

2. Most of us are different sizes from top to bottom. For example, you may be a 6 on top but a 12 on the bottom. Many stores will mix and match two-piece suits for you.

3. If you're flat-chested, strapless styles are good. "Full-figured gals," as Jane Russell used to say, look best in underwire or tops with straps going over the shoulders, or tied back at the neck. If you've got it, flaunt it!

Figure 7-23 Bathing Suits.

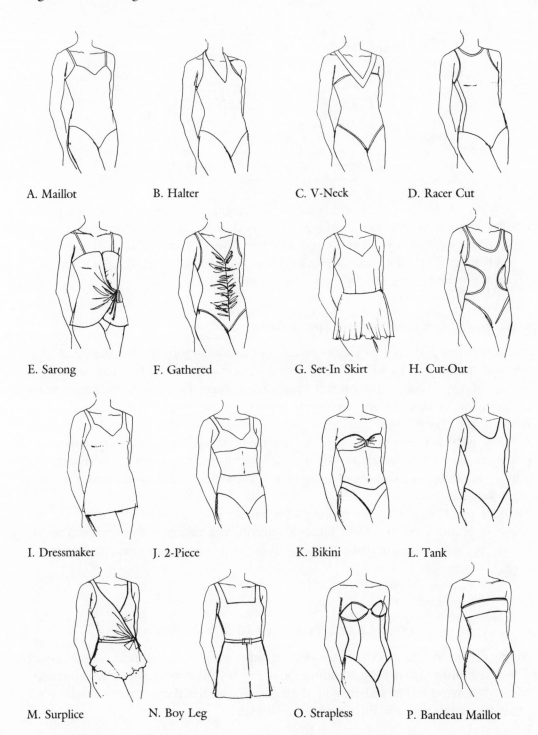

A. Maillot   B. Halter   C. V-Neck   D. Racer Cut

E. Sarong   F. Gathered   G. Set-In Skirt   H. Cut-Out

I. Dressmaker   J. 2-Piece   K. Bikini   L. Tank

M. Surplice   N. Boy Leg   O. Strapless   P. Bandeau Maillot

Figure 7-23 (Continued)

Q. Blouson   R. French Cut

4. Bathing suit bottoms (2-piece, bikini) can be a nightmare if they don't fit properly. Unless you've got a perfect set of buns, don't buy a G-string style, or one that creeps up and looks like one. Even 1-piece suits have bottom elastics that need constant readjusting. Keep trying on different suits until you find one which fits and does not need constant tugging and pulling to stay in place.

Special Notes on Activewear and Sports Attire

Activewear refers not only to jogging suits, but to all clothing that is designed with sports and mobility in mind. It can be worn all year round, and for many occasions other than sports. Some activewear is treated with appliqué, faux jewels, and other pretty embellishments or designs, and will rarely be seen on the tennis court, but rather at a party, or while cruising trendy shops.

Petite activewear pieces have been scaled down to eliminate bulk and to give a shapelier appearance. Elastic waistbands are slightly narrower in petite activewear, and pants are less likely to droop like diapers, which is enough to make any self-respecting woman give up jogging!

Spandex and lycra clothes are making a big impact in all areas of activewear and are available in petite sizes, too. Most bodysuits and bicycle racing outfits conform to the body, so you must take care that pants lengths are short enough to guarantee a smooth look.

WEDDING DRESSES

Wedding dresses are supposed to transform you into a vision of loveliness on that special day, but truthfully, the wrong wedding dress can be a disaster, especially on petites. Yards of billowing fabric and full-cut skirts, as well as the shiny texture or the stark white color many are made in, are often unflattering.

Petite wedding dresses fit beautifully and save costly alterations, but it's really best to know what style looks best for your body type. Here are some helpful hints:

1. **Top heavy**: Emphasize your waistline and avoid high necklines, as well as tiny tucks and frills that are narrow. A scooped neckline with a wide frill in an on- or off-the-shoulder look is good. Keep sleeves narrow to de-emphasize the upper body.
2. **Short waisted**: Avoid a fitted bodice or wide sash treatment. A dropped-waist dress would be ideal.
3. **Long waisted**: An empire style gown is a good choice. Stay away from fussy waist treatment and narrow sleeves. Keep detail on upper part of body—no flowers or frills on the hemline.
4. **Pear shaped**: Keep the emphasis on the upper part of the body, away from the hips. A low V- or scooped neckline trimmed with wide lace and full elbow-length sleeves trimmed with lace is ideal. Don't let detail get fussy—any detail on the skirt should be on or near the hemline, *not* on the hip!
5. **Hourglass**: A shaped, fitted dress with equal proportion on top and bottom is good. High necks, Edwardian style of lace or frills is pretty. Keep the fabric simple. Sleeves should be slightly full, tapering into the waist, with fitted bodice treatments, full skirts, and pretty sash treatments. Keep lace trim on the narrow side.

Choosing the wedding dress that's best for you is confusing and time-consuming without a little planning. Begin by looking through bridal magazines and go to bridal shops and look around. Talk to the salespeople and try on every style you can, whether you think it will look good or not, because you'll make a better choice through the simple process of elimination. Many women want to project a certain image, but often choose a gown that's inappropriate, sometimes with the help of a salesperson who is on commission!

The finest dresses are made of fine, delicate fabrics—voile, silk and satin charmeuse, lace, taffeta, and battiste weight cotton for summer—and are too expensive to risk making a mistake on anything but a dress you **love**.

Many brides have themes for the wedding, depending on style or time of year—although white is traditionally worn, soft creams or pale ivories may look better with your color "season."

A "going-away" outfit is the last vestige of the traditional trousseau. Keep it simple —a suit or silk dress is appropriate and can be worn again!

Your veil or headdress is your most important accessory, especially if you're petite. Short, stiff veils and broad-brimmed hats will cut your height considerably. Instead, choose longer, softer, lacy veils and hats with small upturned brims, Juliet caps, or pretty English-style bowlers (similar to old-fashioned ladies' riding hats) with frothy veil treatments. Silk or fresh flower garlands or headbands are lovely, too. A few weeks before the wedding, go to your hair stylist so that you can plan how you'll wear your hair ahead of time—you'll be nervous enough on the big day without worrying about your hair or makeup. Since white or off-white clothing washes out your complexion, have a professional makeover done to plan (and buy) the most flattering cosmetics to complete your look.

Gloves are optional—they're usually worn only for formal weddings. Pick fingerless styles (you'll have to get the ring on!) in lace or fine fabric.

Shoes are practically unnoticeable under a floor-length dress. Satin shoes in creamy white or ivory are best, and can be dyed beautifully in colors matching the bridesmaids' dresses. Above all, make sure your shoes are comfortable and *not* too high. You don't want to "teeter" gingerly up and down the aisle, and you'll be on your feet a great deal during the reception. I won't make any jokes about getting "cold feet"—everyone has them a little bit. If you're going to wear open toe shoes or sandals, please have a perfect pedicure and wear sheer-toed hose!

Jewelry should be conservative and kept to a minimum. Pearls, diamonds and semi-precious stones for earrings (drops or studs), pearl necklaces and delicate pendants or crosses are all very appropriate. Tailor jewelry to the shape of your dress' neckline treatment.

With all of the frou-frou on you, the groom is not to be forgotten, not now, and not "from this day forward." His clothes should harmonize with yours and the rest of the wedding party. Just make sure he's not wearing more ruffles than you are, and keep cuff links, ties, and boutonieres elegant and understated.

A little thought and a lot of careful planning before the wedding will make this important occasion go smoothly. Looking at your wedding pictures later on, you'll be struck by the fact that your clothes will take second place to the happy faces of those surrounding you on your special day.

MATERNITY

Fashion obviously won't be your top priority at this time, but you'll want to feel stylish as well as comfortable, so here are some things to remember:

1. You may be "showing" for more than one season, in more than one type of weather.
2. You'll wear the same clothes over and over.
3. Petites also show weight gain far more quickly than taller women, so you'll have to dress with special attention to details that elongate.
4. Make a list of the things in your wardrobe that you can wear throughout most or all of your pregnancy—cardigans, some coats and jackets, etc.
5. Buy or make one or two simple, basic dresses or jumpers that will go with blouses (unbuttoned at the bottom), sweaters, jackets, scarves, and other accessories you already own. If the last three or four months of your pregnancy will occur during more than

one season, choose lightweight fabrics, as you can warm them up with shawls and sweaters, while you cannot cool down heavy fabrics.

6. Maternity pants and skirts are great wardrobe extenders, as they will work with a variety of tops.

7. The late Princess Grace said that during her pregnancies she brought all the attention to her face by using scarves at the neckline, and brighter makeup colors to draw the eye to her face, and away from her midsection.

8. Feet tend to swell during pregnancy, sometimes remaining slightly larger permanently! This is, therefore, no time for high heels, which will make the swelling worse, and put additional strain on the already strained back. Remember, too, that you will also want support hose, both for comfort, and to help forestall varicose veins. My mom swears that she kept her figure by wearing a girdle, and also recommends a support bra, but that is a matter of personal comfort.

8

ALL ABOUT ACCESSORIES

Accessories can make or break an outfit. Accessories should harmonize and look appropriate. It's best to begin building up a selection of basic pieces first, adding trendy things later.

Petites have to scale their accessories as carefully as their clothes. Large, chunky, wide pieces will make us look the same way.

Accessories will last a long time if you always buy the best quality in materials and workmanship. Classic styles date less quickly than novelty designs. Always keep shoes, belts, and bags maintained with regular visits to the repair shop.

Accessories can:

- Make your wardrobe seem larger.
- Update your basics.
- Add color or splash.
- Focus the eye for emphasis where *you* want it.
- Take you from office to smart soirées in a jiffy.

Accessories should be thought of in two categories:

Investment	Statement
Fine Handbags	Scarves, Shawls, Sashes
Fine Jewelry	Costume Jewelry
Good Belts	Hats/Hair Doodads
Good Shoes	Flowers
Good Gloves	Colored Gloves, Hose, Belts

Clearly, some statement accessories can be inexpensive "this year" update items. But the bulk of your accessory dollar should be put into investment items. Women on budgets (who isn't?) may benefit from compiling a "wish list" and tackling this collection over a period of years, through sales and special offerings.

SHOES

The human foot contains 26 bones, 107 ligaments, and 19 muscles. The average person will walk over 100,000 miles in his or her lifetime. The wrong shoe fit, poor workmanship, and cheap materials can ruin feet fast. Here are tips on buying quality footwear.

Leather is finely grained and supple and can bend and flex. Uppers are lightweight leather, while soles are layered leather. The bed, or "last" of the shoe determines overall comfort. There should be a natural slope in the last similar to the curve of your foot. Try shoes from different designers to determine which last is the most comfortable for your feet.

Figure 8-1 *Shoes and boots.*

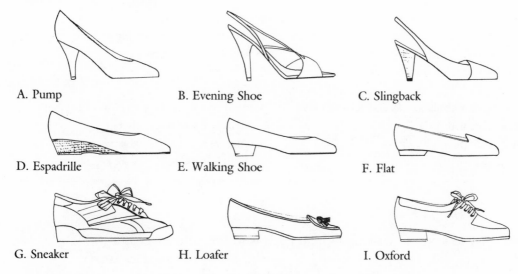

A. Pump   B. Evening Shoe   C. Slingback

D. Espadrille   E. Walking Shoe   F. Flat

G. Sneaker   H. Loafer   I. Oxford

Figure 8-1 (Continued)

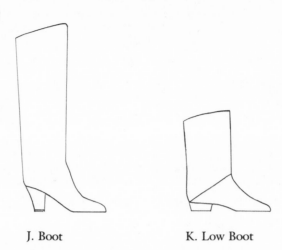

J. Boot   K. Low Boot

Shoe seams should lie flat and show no trace of glue. The welt, a thin strip running fully or partway around part of the shoe, is what holds the upper, insole, and outer sole together, so make sure that it is well-constructed.

Shoe and boot linings should be made of leather, keeping feet warm in winter and cool in summer. Add thermal or shearling liners to absorb, cushion, or warm feet.

Shoes demand the same careful consideration as other wardrobe choices, as the wrong shoes can draw the eye downward, or cut you off, visually, at the ankle, reducing the illusion of height (Figure 8-1).

Here are some tips on shopping for shoes:

Do	Don't
1. Pick neutral colors	1. Wear heels of extreme height
2. Choose heels of medium height	2. Buy T- or ankle straps
3. Wear illusion heels or flat shoes	3. Wear strappy, cut-out styles if you have fat feet
4. Experiment with slingbacks and keyhole toes for comfort with style	4. Wear shoes with bright colors or colored appliques if your feet are big.
5. Wear suede pumps for day or evening	5. Squeeze into narrow shoes with pointed toes —slightly rounded toes are better

Walking in Heels

"The secret to walking in high heels is to keep the knees straight."

—BIANCA JAGGER

HOSIERY

Here are some helpful hints for choosing hosiery:

1. Match **hosiery to shoe** color for a longer line.
2. **Wash new hose** before you wear them; they won't run as quickly.
3. Petites should keep patterns, lace, and detail delicate and small in **scale**.
4. **Seamed and unseamed** stockings worn with garter belts are coming back into fashion. Wear them under classic, tailored clothes to feel super-feminine!
5. **Heavy legs** look best in dark hose, with a slightly flaring hemline at the knee.
6. **Thin legs** can take light, pale hose with a straight skirt, tapered hemline.
7. **Support** hose now comes in sheer textures and pretty shades. Consider it if you do a great deal of standing or have circulation problems.
8. Hose in **colors** other than that of your skin can be used in many ways to create fashion "looks." Colored hose are easy to use and give the wearer "the finished leg" (Figure 8-2).

Figure 8-2 *There are four ways to use fashion color hose:*

A. **Neutral** hose—skin color, or close to it.

B. Hose **matching** skirt and shoes. (This is the overall most elongating and slimming treatment.)

C. Hose **contrasting** hem and shoe. (This treatment visually shortens the lower leg.)

D. **Hose and shoe** contrasting hem color. (This treatment visually elongates the lower leg.)

9. **Never** wear hose that are snug across the thigh. Slit seams in the thigh and/or crotch area can be agony by day's end.

10. **High heels and sandals** with high heels require sheer hose. Many sheer hose, however, are now available in fashion colors, so you can use dressy hose in the same ways (*see* Figure 8-2) that you would use daytime hose.

HANDBAGS

Most of us use large, practical bags for school or work. For petites, in particular, this can be a fashion blunder on two fronts. One, the proportion of a great, big bag on a small woman is invariably wrong. Two, heavy bags are bad for the spine. An excellent and fashionable solution is to carry two bags, one on each side, such as a tote and an envelope bag, or a tailored bag and a light attaché. Other handbag tips are:

1. Small clutch and metal minaudières are elegant for evening. They can be expensive, so you may wish to haunt postholiday sales to find one good evening bag.

2. Straps on shoulder bags should be kept shorter on petites, so that they don't hang too low. For security reasons, do not let shoulder bags dangle behind your back.

3. Neutrals are your best investment if your budget is limited. Neutrals are not only beige, brown, black, gray, white, navy and taupe, but red, which goes with almost everything.

4. Handbags do not have to match your shoes—that is an old rule, long since disregarded by the fashion industry.

5. Make sure the bag will hold your usual purse contents without looking like an overripe melon. Purse organizers are great, not only because they make changing from one bag to another a snap, but because they make it simple for you to try your contents in a new bag you are considering. Some stores take a dim view of your dumping the messy contents of your bag all over the counter.

BELTS

Here are some tips on belts:

1. Keep belts medium to narrow in width with simple buckle treatments. Add interest with different leathers and fabrics. Add glitz or accessory detail to belts only if you have a small waist. Never wear large belts if you're short-waisted. Try cummerbunds in leather, suede, or silk, or scarves tied creatively in place of a traditional belt.

2. Try blousing over your belt to hide a thick or short waist. Your local cobbler can add extra holes to your belts if necessary.

3. All belts, cummerbunds, sashes, and contrast waist colors should be medium-scaled,

not large. Match your belt color to your top if you're short-waisted, and to your bottom if you're long-waisted, to achieve a proportioned look.

HATS

Hats can look great on everyone. Petites look best in small, "cocktail size" hats with scaled brims, poms, veils, and trims. Cocktail hats are not appropriate for daytime wear. Here are some guidelines:

1. Always look inside the hat to determine which is the back (the label or seam is at the back). When trying on the hat, try it in various positions, for example, pulled far down to the brow for a high fashion look or tilted to the side for a jaunty and face-slimming look. Don't forget to check the profile and back view to see how it looks from all angles.

2. Choose hats that flatter the shape of your face; *i.e.*, round hats on angular faces, small, close brims on narrow faces, and height-creating turbans and pillboxes on round or wide faces.

3. Match a wool hat to gloves and a scarf to work with a favorite coat or coats to create an outerwear "ensemble."

4. The phrase "old hat" holds true only if the hat has not been properly protected. Store hats in tissue paper in hat boxes or on stands. When a hat is really "shot," throw it out, or use it for gardening.

5. Another phrase, "as exciting as last year's hat" applies to hats that are very trendy, so if you wish to wear a hat for several years, choose a classic style (Figure 8-3).

Figure 8-3 *Hats should never be wider than your shoulders or less narrow than your hairdo.*

SCARVES

Good scarves never seem to go out of style, can be worn all year long, and come in a variety of sizes, shapes, and fabrics. There are a number of booklets on the subject of scarf tying, many of them free at the scarf counter of your local department store. Build a wardrobe of scarves in your favorite colors and in varied designs and fabrics.

There are many ways to work with scarves, but these are 20 of my favorites, including one technique, "The Vogel Knot," which has been created exclusively for *The Complete Petite* (Figure 8-4).

Figure 8-4 *Twenty ways to tie a scarf.*

1. *Inside Knot*

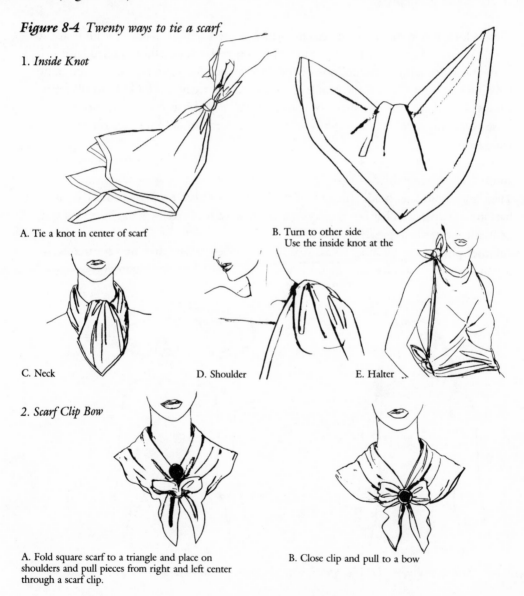

A. Tie a knot in center of scarf

B. Turn to other side
Use the inside knot at the

C. Neck   D. Shoulder   E. Halter

2. *Scarf Clip Bow*

A. Fold square scarf to a triangle and place on shoulders and pull pieces from right and left center through a scarf clip.

B. Close clip and pull to a bow

3. *The Pilgrim*

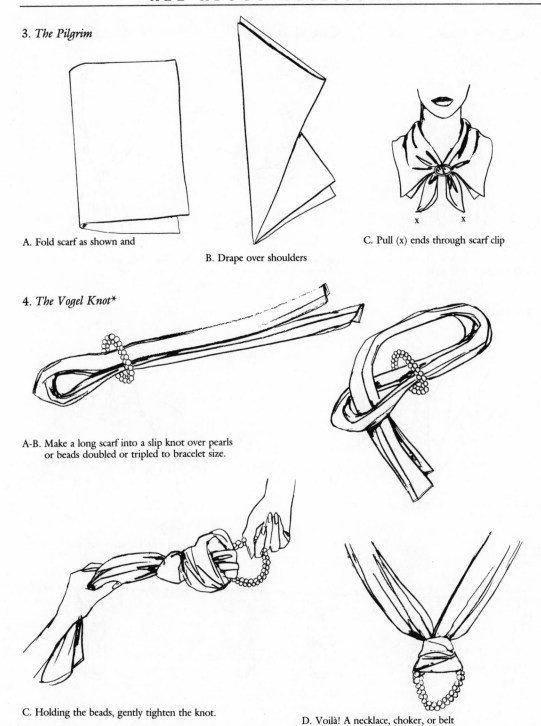

A. Fold scarf as shown and

B. Drape over shoulders

C. Pull (x) ends through scarf clip

4. *The Vogel Knot**

A-B. Make a long scarf into a slip knot over pearls
   or beads doubled or tripled to bracelet size.

C. Holding the beads, gently tighten the knot.

D. Voilà! A necklace, choker, or belt

* This is a *Complete Petite* "original" from Sue Vogel.

5. *The Shoulder Drape*

Halve and drape a large scarf or shawl. Fasten underneath with a pin.

6. *The Bandito*

Halve a small square and knot at the nape.

7. *The Portrait*

Tie a long scarf in a low knot or square knot.

8. *The Hankie*

Quarter a small lace hankie and pin to a shoulder or lapel.

9. *The Cocoon*

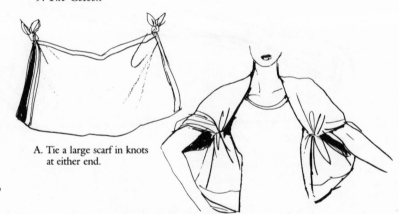

A. Tie a large scarf in knots at either end.

B. Slip over arms with knots towards the front— chic!

10. *The Lady Tie*

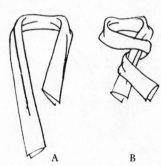  

A   B   C   D

E. Slip pearls or beads through the square knot.

A-D. Make a long thin scarf into a classic tie.

11. *The Necklace*

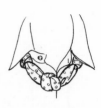

A-B. Take a long thin scarf or a square folded to a thinner diagonal and twist and knot.

C. Extra knots will shorten

D. Place at the neck and tie at the back. (P.S. This is also a great "headband.")

12. *The Ascot*

A. Bring a long thin scarf around the neck as shown

B. Slip one side neatly over the other—a pin or flower makes a pretty fastener.

13. *The Rosette*

A. Tie a thin scarf around the neck (waist or head) and twist the ends.

B. Twist the twisted ends into a circle.

C. Catch the ends underneath the rosette.

14. *The Turban or Choke*

A. Knot the center of a long scarf once or twice.

B. Place the knot at the throat and tie in back.

C. Or, tie it at the back of the hair for a turban look.

15. *The Fling*

A. Drape a thin scarf around the shoulders.   B. Slip one end over the other.   C. Hold the ends down with pearls or beads.

16. *Side Pouf*

A. Tie a single knot with one end twice as long as the other.   B. Make a bow loop of the longer end.   C. Fluff out the loop.

17. *The Grace Kelly*

Fold a square into a large triangle and tie around hair to the back of the neck. This works best with a chiffon scarf and sunglasses.

18. *The Pleated Jabot*

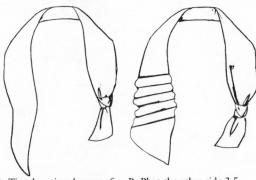  

A. Tie a knot in a long scarf.

B. Pleat the other side 3-5 times.

C. Slip one side of the pleats through the knot.

D. Pull the knot taut and fluff both pleated sides.

19. *The Turban Wrap*

A. Tie a long thin scarf or sash as shown and twist 2 or 3 times.

B. Bring the ends to the back of the neck and tie or tuck into the sides.

20. *The Crochet Tie*

A. Make a loop

B. Begin a chain stitch

C. Continue chain until the scarf or sash is the length you wish.

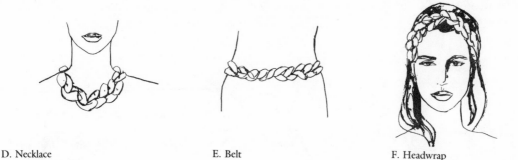

D. Necklace   E. Belt   F. Headwrap

GLOVES

Not so long ago, women were considered "half-dressed" without their gloves. Today, that only holds true for the Arctic Circle. However, gloves enhance outfits and, like fashion hosiery, often give that finished, polished look to an outfit with relatively little fuss, and without your spending a fortune. In short, a simple pair of gloves can go a long way. Gloves not only keep your hands clean and warm, they give you a better grip and hide expensive jewelry. Here are some guidelines:

1. For daytime wear choose flexible, strong, fine leather, either pigskin or suede, with wool or cashmere linings.
2. For summer or formal affairs, try lace, fishnet, or fine cotton gloves.
3. For evening, try suede, velveteen, or satin jersey; they add a touch of elegance.

JEWELRY

"Jewelry draws attention to and not away from the face. If your features aren't good, don't wear unnecessary jewelry. You have to proportion jewelry to your face as you do for clothes. Evening jewelry and hair ornaments can go bolder on petites, but must not overpower."

—KATHRYN LEE, 5'3"
JEWELRY AND ACCESSORY DESIGNER

Most people feel that it is better to rely on a few good pieces than to wear lots of faddish clutter. This is particularly important to the petite, as jewelry should always be in proportion to its wearer. Here are some other guidelines:

1. If you have a full face or thick neck, don't wear thin, delicate jewelry.
2. Wear chokers and multiple strand necklaces if you have a slim or long neck.
3. Avoid dangles and big hoops, as they can be overpowering.
4. Pair delicate cameos and brooches with tweeds and wools.
5. Experiment with new textures, materials, and designs such as tortoiseshell, wood, plastic, fabric, papier-mâché, or handcrafted, one-of-a-kind pieces such as "wearable art."
6. Pick earrings that mimic the size and scale of your face.
7. Here are some special notes on pearls and oysters:
   a. Match pearl color to the color of your teeth to keep your smile looking bright.
   b. Wear real pearls often to keep them from calcifying and breaking down.
   c. A **choker** is the shortest necklace, sometimes several strands thick, and looks best on thin necks.
   d. A **princess** length ends about 3″ below the base of the neck, and can be worn by anyone.
   e. **Matinee** strands end at the breastbone, and can be worn by anyone who is not terribly buxom.
   f. **Opera** length ends at the low midriff, and is especially good for petites, as it is an elongating length.
   g. A **rope** goes past the waist, and can overwhelm the petite woman. This is a very dramatic look.
   h. **Graduated pearls** are not the best look for petite women, as they tend to draw the eye down, not up.

Last, but not least, when planning your accessories, don't forget these:

- Lace or linen collars
- Sunglasses
- Silk flowers
- Hair ornaments

However, you should should also be aware when enough is enough—or when enough is too much.

We've all heard "less is more" and "when in doubt, don't."

On the other hand, most of the women I see are wearing too few accessories, thereby making their outfits seem a bit dull. Most women, I believe, leave perfectly good accessories at home in the drawer or closet for fear of looking overdone. Therefore, I have developed this point system, which may seem time-consuming at first, but which will become confidence-engendering second nature to you in no time.

ACCESSORY POINT SYSTEM

Give your outfit *one* point for each of the following:

_____	Earrings
_____	Any other piece of jewelry
_____	Scarf
_____	Flower
_____	Hat
_____	Gloves
_____	Brightly manicured hands (red, hot pink, orange, or very long [ugh!] nails)
_____	Major makeup
_____	Glasses or sunglasses
_____	Each pattern, stripe, or major visible texture
_____	Each outstanding trim: embroidery, shiny buttons, emblems, contrast braid, etc.
_____	Startling or contrasting belt
_____	Contrast or startling handbag
_____	Eye-catching hose
_____	TOTAL

Now, total up the number of points.

SCORING
   Five or less is probably dull!
   Six to ten is exciting and eye-catching!!
   Eleven or more is too much!!!

Last, but not least, check the placement of your accessories. Are the emphasis points correct for you? Are you drawing attention to those traits or parts of the body you wish to emphasize?

Yes? Then, go out and dazzle them!

9

BUILDING A WARDROBE

If you have put so much as one baby toe into the wonderful world of image consulting, color analysis, or (the latest rage) **total imaging**, you may have heard enough about building a wardrobe to give you the MEGO Syndrome (*My Eyes Glaze Over*). Unless, however, you can honestly say that you always have something wonderful to wear for each occasion that pops up, **you must** come to grips with the wardrobe that you have versus the one that you want.

REVIEWING YOUR CURRENT WARDROBE

Using the knowledge you have acquired so far, you will need to re-examine your wardrobe and see if any of the following apply:

- You have lots of clothes, but sometimes, nothing to wear.
- You sometimes feel self-conscious in your clothes.
- You shop haphazardly or impulsively with no real sense of purpose of an overall plan, or of what you need.

- You have been known to spend more than you can afford *or* you only buy on sale. ("This whole outfit only cost me $6.99!")
- Nothing in your closet seems to go together. It's hard to assemble outfits.
- You have more clothes than you can keep track of. Alterations, dry cleaning, organization, and storage seem overwhelming.
- You rarely receive compliments on your clothes from others.
- You rely on the advice of family or friends when you buy. You never shop alone, and avoid asking salespeople for help in choosing garments.
- You're not really sure what really suits you, so you buy trendy clothes and change your look frequently to suit the clothes.
- You sometimes/often feel inappropriately dressed for the occasion.
- You've never bothered to shop the Petite Departments, still believing that regular sizes fit you just as well.

FOUR-STEP PROCEDURE FOR PLANNING YOUR PERFECT WARDROBE

Whether you're dissatisfied with what you have and want to start finding new pieces, or need guidelines to find things that become you, planning a wardrobe is easy if you use this four-step procedure.

1. Make a list of every item you have. Divide the list into dresses, suits, sportswear, coats, lingerie, evening wear, and accessories.
2. Discard clothes you never wear (vintage and very special evening gowns excepted)—anything that's uncomfortable, unflattering in color or style or doesn't fit. Give them to consignment or thrift shops, or donate them to the Salvation Army; they'll give you a tax credit receipt.
3. Check over what's left to see if alterations or repairs are needed, and have the tailoring done professionally if you can't sew. Examine shoulder pads, pleats, tucking, and hemlines and freshen them up.
4. Always keep your clothes clean, in top condition and ready to wear. As a commercial actress, I often need a suit for corporate-style jobs, or "young mother" outfits for the "homey" touch. Sometimes I change several times a day, so I work on having my things clean and pressed!

Remember, when assembling your wardrobe, it is extremely important to keep in mind your style or the "look" that you are trying to achieve. The three most common looks which women try to achieve are: **classic, trendy**, or **fashion**. The following chart will give examples of the types of purchases each one of those three looks might require.

It will also illustrate my point that you need to spend a vast amount of money to have all looks in your closet at once. **Know your "look" before you buy!**

A LITTLE "LOOK" CHART

	Classic	Trendy	Fashion
Jackets	Longer jacket lengths, double breasted, subtle colors, patterns	Mandarin, shawl, jewel neck treatments	Big shoulder pads, curvy waists
Skirts	Slim, knee- or longer length, dirndl, knife or box pleats	Mix or contrast colors, shorter or mini skirts	Knee length or shorter skirts, or very long skirts
Handbags	Clutch, envelope, briefcase, conservative colors	Big shoulder bags, suede and leather mixes, school bags, clear colors, pastels	Chanel type bags, small shoulder bags, designer handbags
Jewelry	Pearls, chains, pendants, small pins	Big, bold jewelry, newest style, costume jewelry	Good fakes, the "real thing"
Hats and Hair Ornaments	Beret, pillbox, velvet bows or hairbands	Outrageous hat (You'll know **it** when you see it!)	Chanel bows, snoods, scarf treatments, braids, and hairpieces

Having determined your "look" and put your existing wardrobe in order, you are now ready to plan what you are going to add in the next year, or season, if you find it easier to think in seasons. Using the list you made for Step 1, do the following;

A. Decide what you need by category: dresses, coats, blouses, etc., and, if possible, decide in what colors. Call this your Master Shopping List (MSL).
B. Put a mark next to each item on your list of currently owned clothes for those items that are appropriate for:
    H   At home
    W   At work (paid or volunteer—out of the home)
    D   Dressy or formal
    S   Sports or hobbies
    O   Out and about (shopping, errands, hanging out, etc.)

Review your Lifestyle Quiz in Chapter 5. **Is your wardrobe as it exists now in** proportion to your lifestyle needs, and to the types of things you spend your time doing during the daytime, weekend, and evening? If not, **alter** your MSL.

SECRETS OF THE CAPSULE WARDROBE

Whether you are beginning a Wardrobe (you can spell it with a capital "W" when you put time, planning, and effort into it) or adding to one you have already built, your best bet is to learn the **Capsule Wardrobe** trick. A capsule wardrobe consists of five to ten pieces in two or three harmonious colors of your choice, which, in turn, mix and match to create endless combinations and permutations of outfits.

Here's how a capsule works:
Say you buy:

1. Black jacket
2. Black skirt
3. Red shirtdress
4. Black, red, and white print 2-piece dress
5. White V-neck sweater

How many outfits can you make? 1 + 2 + 4 (top); 1 + 2 + 5; 1 + 3; 1 + 4; 4(bottom) + 5; 2 + 5; 1 + 4; 1 + 3; 2 + 4(top) + 5, and more. . . .
Now, say you find that you already have in your closet:

6. Red shawl
7. White blouse
8. Black pants
9. White skirt
10. Red sweater-vest

Now how many outfits can you make? Think of the added potential from the shawl alone—not only as a shawl, but as a halter under the black jacket, or as a hip sash over the print skirt, etc. Not to mention the bright pink blouse you already own, with the black jacket and skirt, et cetera, et cetera, et cetera, as the King of Siam would say.

Capsule Wardrobes are wonderful in and of themselves. Year after year, however, they grow in your closet to intermingle with each other, and in no time flat, you find yourself no longer bored by the necessity of wearing the "same old thing" again. This is better than a new twist on meatloaf!

Here are some rough formulas for buying a business or a casual **capsule wardrobe**:

	Business	Casual
Color 1	Jacket	Cardigan
	Skirt	Pants
Color 2	Print skirt and blouse	Print skirt and top
Color 3	Blouse	V-neck shell/vest
OPTIONAL:		
Color 1	Shell	Short sleeve sweater
Color 2		Scarf
Color 3	2-piece shirtdress	Shirt
	Shawl	Pants

Once you have a master list, your shopping habits should change as you develop a sense of organization, which you may have previously lacked. Some women say that they like to carry a small copy of this list in their wallets. Just remember to update the list as you review the four steps of the wardrobe planning process each season.

DRESSING FOR THE JOB INTERVIEW

Last, but not least, I have included some simple suggestions for that most dreaded of all occasions, the job interview. So much has been said on this subject—"Which outfit got the job?, or Why Sally's outfit cost her the job," that one might think that a job interview was a new name for a fashion show. In fact, clothing choices are only important in three ways:

1. Your clothes should make you feel comfortable and confident.
2. Your clothes should fit in with the company image.
3. Your clothes should show that you have the good judgment and savvy to know what is correct for this occasion.

Once properly dressed, however, it does help to have prepared for the interview by learning as much as you can about the company and the job. There are many books written about what to do and say on the job interview, and I recommend that you enhance your confidence by reading one. From the many women I know who have approached the job search with a great enthusiasm, I have made this list of questions you are likely to be asked on an interview:

- What is your greatest weakness?
- What is your greatest strength?
- Why have you switched jobs so often?
- Why do you think we should hire you?
- What are you looking for out of life?
- When are you going to have children, or what will you do if your kids are sick on a day when we need you?
- What is your greatest accomplishment?

Good answers are short and positive, and **never** defensive. Your greatest weakness should be something like your perfectionism on the job, or tendency to work too hard. No matter what, remain cool. This is, further, no time for political debates relating to the role of women in the workforce. And while we all resent the questions that only women are asked about intentions for having and rearing a family, statistics do show that women with small children need more personal time than single women, so keep in mind that your interviewer may be simply trying to ascertain your talents with the best interests of the company in mind. Remember the wise words of a friend of mine who says she goes on every job interview determined to like everyone, and to get an offer. Later, she can turn it down, if she chooses, but only if she wins at the interview game in the first place.

For the petite woman, behavior and appearance on the interview are particularly important. Many people still think we are more cute than serious, and as unfair as that prejudice may be, you will be best off to take my advice. Consider it your mission on the job interview to overcome all objections, and to get that job!

Some last advice for when you are "on the grill":

- Keep in mind that the first 30 seconds in which someone meets you at a job interview creates the lasting impression they will forever have of you, until you prove otherwise.
- Even if the position you're seeking will entail wearing a uniform (the armed services excepted), your clothes will speak volumes for you if they are neat and clean.
- Dress in a manner that you'll be able to maintain if you get the job. A dress or separates in neutral or warm colors, light navy or gray, or subtle patterns are good choices. Bring in any highlight colors with accessories. Take a spare pair of hose in case you get a run. Shoes should be understated with a medium heel. Keep jewelry simple and uncluttered. Dangling earrings and jangling bracelets do not foster employer confidence.
- Any briefcase or handbag you bring along should be of good quality and in good condition.

• Keep makeup fresh and to a minimum. Hair should be clean, neat, and unfussy. Hands and nails should be manicured.

Put yourself in the employer's place and think about what you'd like to see in a potential employee. Looking good makes you feel self-assured and projects the confidence you'll need to land that job! **Go for it!**

For the petite woman starting in the *Mondo Corporato*, building and maintaining a wardrobe of good suits is slow and expensive. I therefore made up the following chart in the hope that it may be helpful in planning your suit and blouse wardrobe for maximum versatility.

SUIT COLORS

	White	Gray	Charcoal	Brown	Black	Navy	Red	Beige	Tan
TOPS									
White	x	x	x	x	x	x	x	x	x
Pastel		x	x	x		x		x	
Bright	x	x	x		x	x		x	x
Beige				x	x	x	x	x	x
Gray	x	x	x	x			x		
Red	x	x	x	x	x	x		x	x
Navy	x					x	x		
Black	x	x			x		x	x	

10

MODEL TIPS:
ICING THE CAKE

Many women mistakenly think that models and actresses are born beautiful while they themselves are born hopeless.

Every woman should remember that **grooming, posture,** and **voice** are as important today as they ever were in an 19th-century etiquette book.

GROOMING

Good grooming consists of continual upkeep with:

- Soap and water
- Toothpaste, floss, and mouthwash
- Deodorants
- Superfluous hair removers

These items are not only the tools of good grooming, but the *sine qua non* of a modern civilized person. Grooming is simple once you learn to make a **personal routine** for yourself. Begin with cleanliness, a daily bath or shower, and one other key ingredient that models know about, a good night's sleep. Well-rested people not only look better, but tend to be more happy, cheerful, and positive. The French call the daily grooming *la toilette*. Each woman should create her own grooming schedule. The following guidelines will help you to do this.

HAIR REMOVAL

For most women, removal of superfluous hair is a basic grooming issue. Waxing, shaving, depilatory, and electrolysis all have their good and bad points, but for the moment, that's all there is. The following chart may help you decide what is best for you.

Method	Pro	Con
Shaving	Convenient, fast, easy, and close	Nicks, rashes, ingrown hairs, stubble within 24 hours
Electric Razor	Easy, fast, safe Rashes are less common	Less close shave than razor, needs to be done more often
Depilatories	Longer lasting than razor, smooth	Expensive, smelly, abrasive, rashes, and ingrown hairs, hard to keep in control—so on the bikini area, can be overdone, resulting in a mohawk!
Waxing or any pull-out machine	Fast, lasts for weeks, smooth	Painful, and expensive; redness for 24–48 hours
Electrolysis	Permanent	Slow, time-consuming and expensive, rash for 48 hours. Often has to be done over and over to be permanent; rare pitting of the skin.
Epilady and other hair root removal shavers, or tweezing	Lasts for weeks, smooth	Painful, ingrown hairs occasionally

SKIN CARE

There are five basic rules for keeping skin soft and youthful. Follow them and you will have skin that others will envy:

1. No woman should expose her skin to the **sun** for more than five minutes without protection. There has been an increase in skin cancer even in teenagers. Perhaps our vanishing ozone layer is to blame. In any case, wear sunglasses, hats, and strong sunblocks when you must be in the sun. If bathing in the sun is your favorite hobby, find a new pastime.
2. Do not **touch your face** with your hands. The germs on your hands can infect your pores and cause blemishes. Ditto, the telephone; clean it often with rubbing alcohol to reduce chin blemishes.
3. Unless you're a stand-up comedienne, don't **grimace, scowl**, or **mug**. Not only do these gestures cause unattractive lines, but they give you a very unpoised look.
4. **Eat properly**, drink a lot of water, don't smoke, and don't drink alcohol.
5. Become religious about the morning and evening **cleansing** of your face and neck. You cannot neglect your face for weeks and then have a great facial, and expect to have good skin.

It is said, **you are what you eat**. There are certain foods that are very popular among models and other women who are good looking for a living. Eat the following foods as a replacement for the usual grease-burger and chips, and watch your skin texture and general glow improve:

- **Carrots** for vitamin A, which improves eyesight and promotes good absorption of other vitamins, like C.
- **Tomatoes** for vitamin A.
- **Green peppers** for vitamin C, which helps fight colds and gum or skin disorders.
- **Parsley** for red blood cells to prevent anemia.
- **Broccoli** for vitamins A and C.
- **Strawberries** for healing, collagen production, and to prevent capillary breakage.
- **Papaya** for vitamin A, calcium, and potassium. It is also good when applied to the face as a masque. Place the peel with inside down on cleansed skin. Lie down for 20 minutes, and then remove the peel to dewy, radiant skin.
- **Oats** to help reduce cholesterol, and also as an exfoliating masque when mixed with water, or with honey and beaten egg, and applied to the skin for 15 minutes, and then removed in a gentle, circular, massaging motion.
- **Chicken** for cell growth and energy, and for niacin, which helps break up cholesterol.
- **Fresh fish** for its highly praised fish oil, and for zinc, very important for good skin and for the prevention of acne.

- **Water**, six or more glasses every day to rid the skin of excess oil, and to promote its natural cleansing.

And another thing . . . teenagers are not the only ones who get acne. Adult acne is caused in large part by stress, and when we become nervous or overwhelmed by our responsibilities. It can become a source of additional stress in and of itself. Here are some suggestions:

1. When you feel stressed out, find ways to relax, whether that be with a book, hobby, music, or something like biofeedback. Stress is a part of modern life, and the sooner you learn to deal with it without being self-destructive, the better.
2. Go to a dermatologist. In addition to prescribing some of the new medications, a doctor can also tell you which over-the-counter medicines and foods may be bad for you.
3. Don't pick at your face. Use hypoallergenic and fragrance-free cosmetics with clean applicators. Keep your hair clean and change your pillowcases twice a week.
4. Drink eight to ten glasses of water a day.
5. If you are prone to clogged pores, avoid dairy products, and eat food containing bran.
6. Exercise, for your skin's circulation, and because sweating releases dirt and built-up oil from the pores.
7. Have professional facials, if you can afford them. If you can't afford them, learn to do the following once or twice a month at home:
   a. Cream your face with vegetable oil
   b. Tissue off the excess
   c. Steam your face for five minutes
   d. Use a facial scrub—oatmeal or salt, with water
   e. Wash thoroughly
   f. Apply astringent with a cotton ball
   g. Apply moisturizer
   h. Steam your face again
   i. Rinse your face with cool water

MAKEUP

Many women think it's a crime to put makeup on beautiful, well-cared-for skin. Wrong! Proper makeup:

- Protects the skin from the environment
- Brightens the face
- Defines the features
- Gives a woman a cared-for look of high self-esteem

• Does **not** get in the way of being perceived as professional, competent, or intelligent

Many women wear no makeup because they don't know how to apply it and don't want to look foolish. The following tips will make it clear that makeup is really a simple art.

Foundation

On clean, toned, and moisturized skin, apply the foundation of your choice. Foundations are either oil base, for dry skin, or water base, for oily skin. Coverage varies from sheer to heavy, depending on the effect you desire. Medium or heavy coverage foundations can be made lighter by applying them with a damp sponge.

Some of the new foundations combine coverage and treatment, in short, looking good while actually benefiting your skin. Foundation can be applied with clean fingers, or with a makeup sponge, which should also be kept clean. Foundation can give a dewy, frosty glow, or be totally matte. In either case, it should be "set" with loose powder with a similar finish, shiny or matte. Powder is best applied with a larger powder brush, and then "set" with a damp, cool face cloth, which removes excess powder and makes the finish last longer.

Make sure you match your natural skin tone perfectly, as there is nothing worse looking than an orange or pink "mask." Foundation should be blended onto the neck and out to the hairline.

*Figure 10-1 Contouring is a tricky skill. Using a makeup base one shade **darker** than usual, apply to the following areas and **blend well.***

A. *Long Face*: Under the cheekbone and at chin

B. *Round Face*: From temple across jaw

C. *Square Face*: From below temple across jaw

D. *Heart-Shaped Face:* From high temple over top of cheekbone

E. *Oval Face*: Under the cheekbone, blended down and back to the jaw

Blusher

I see more mistakes in color and application of blusher than in any other cosmetic. Harsh, dramatic contours and garish colors are artificial and aging. To find a color that is right for you, pinch the end of your finger and look at the color that appears at the tip. Pick your blush a shade lighter for a natural look. To apply, smile, and then apply the blusher on the "apples" of the cheeks. Don't wipe off the excess with a tissue, but apply translucent powder and blend.

Highlighters and contours can work very well on circles, blemishes, double chins, and full cheeks (Figure 10-1).

Lipstick

Lip color should mimic the natural tones of the mouth and cheeks. For a beautiful and long-lasting mouth:

- Moisturize or condition the lips with balm or oil
- Powder the lips lightly
- Apply lip liner
- Apply lip color, blot, and reapply

Forget gloppy lip gloss, but do try some of the new long-lasting or conditioning lipsticks. A soft, flattering color can do a great deal for you, so don't forget to reapply as needed (Figure 10-2).

Figure 10-2 *The six points for shaping your lips.*

Draw a dot with your lip pencil
where each arrow is pointing,
and then "connect the dots."
Fill in with lip pencil and then
fill in with lipstick for a lasting
application.

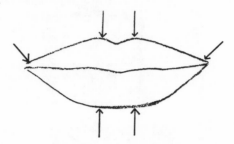

Eye Makeup

The eyes are the most expressive part of your face, and the feature most likely to look amateurish if the eye makeup is applied with a heavy hand or not blended. Eye shadow is really simple if you remember the following:

- Use matte powder shadows—frosted shadows age the eyes and make your eyes look crinkled or wrinkled.
- If you don't like to fuss with eye shadows, try using just one color, a soft neutral like a medium matte brown or taupe.
- If your eye makeup tends to run, use loose powder under your eyes, and colorless mascara instead of, or over your usual mascara. Use liquid eye liner, or eye shadow applied wet with a brush as eye liner, and do not use pencil inside your lower lash line, as this is the number one type of eye makeup which is likely to run, especially in hot weather (Figure 10-3).

Figure 10-3 *Eye shadow technique:*

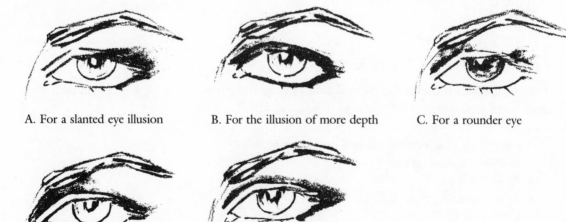

A. For a slanted eye illusion   B. For the illusion of more depth   C. For a rounder eye

D. For a more deeply set illusion   E. For a wider eye

Good daily skin care is absolutely necessary underneath makeup. The best paint job in the world will not look good if it is applied on a bumpy canvas!

Several companies now offer color system makeup, lines of cosmetics that are designed to go together by color. Choose a color family that is most flattering to you, and then stick with it. The colors should range from soft to vibrant in intensity, building from A.M. to P.M. when colors need more punch. Get advice from cosmetics experts before investing in a new line of makeup, as a mistake can be costly. Seasonal color analysis makes makeup easier, and the following chart lists the seasonal basics.

SEASONAL MAKEUP COLORS

Product	Winter	Summer	Spring	Autumn
Blusher	Clear Pink	Soft Rose	Clear Salmon	Chestnut
	Plum Wine	Soft Plum	Warm Pink	Terra-Cotta
Lipstick	True Red	Rose Pink	Peach	Brick Red
	Raspberry Plum	Watermelon Pink	Coral	Cinnamon
	Hot Pink	Red	Pink	Orange
Shadow	Dove Gray	Champagne	Ivory	Champagne
	Charcoal	Dove Gray	Peach	Coffee
	Blue Gray	Steel Gray	Soft Aqua	Sage
	Teal	Soft Pink	Warm Pink	Peach
	Royal	Deep Mauve	Honey	Honey
	Mauve	Plum	Warm Green	Smoky Turquoise

MAKEUP BRUSHES

I discovered the results that good makeup brushes can give after my husband gave me a set for Christmas. Until then, I didn't know what I was missing. The best brushes are made with natural hair, such as fox, sable, and squirrel. Synthetic fibers tend to be a bit stiffer, but some of them are quite good, and the price is significantly less. Basic brushes are (Figure 10-4):

- **Powder Brush**: the biggest brush; used for loose powder
- **Blush Brush**: the wide, rounded brush for powder blush
- **Liner Brush**: a fine-tipped brush for eye liner or for concealer on tiny lines or blemishes
- **Eye Shadow Brush**: a flat brush used for applying and softening eye shadow
- **Rounded-Eye Brush**: a medium-sized brush used to apply eye shadow to the entire lid

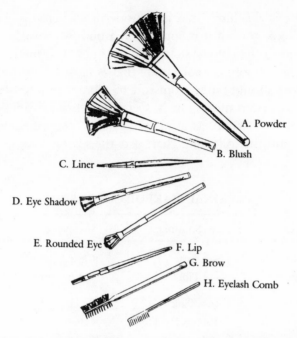

Figure 10-4 The tools of the trade: brushes . . . which, along with makeup sponges, tweezers, lash curlers, pencil sharpeners, swabs, cotton balls, and tissues, should be kept neat and clean, and in easy reach.

- **Lip Brush**: a small brush used to apply lipstick; use the tip to define the shape of the mouth and the flat side to fill in the color
- **Brow Brush**: half brush, half comb, this brush tames the brows and shapes them upward
- **Eyelash Comb**: a comb slightly larger than the brow comb, used immediately after mascara to prevent clumps

These brushes, along with **makeup sponges, eyelash curlers, tweezers, and makeup pencil sharpeners should all be cleaned regularly with shampoo, or with rubbing alcohol mixed with water**.

And, speaking of tweezers, just say **no** to facial hair—it's a big turnoff.

Busy schedules require quick and easy makeup routines. New products on the market can save time and money, and can help you to make even rush jobs look great.

Just as contour and highlight must be used with a light and skillful hand, so should corrective eye and lip makeup. The following chart is designed to give you help in choosing your best eye and lip applications.

Please remember that everyone has features that they would like to change, so you should not dwell on yours, nor should you use makeup to try to dramatically reshape your face, but to make you prettier.

Feature	Description	Correction
Eyes	Close Set	Keep brow corners directly above eye corners. Use light colors, highlight inner eye corner to banish shadows.
	Wide Set	Don't overtweeze brow, especially near the bridge of the nose. Keep lid color at inner corner and center of eye.
	Deep Set	Use light colors and highlight brow bone. Avoid lining or using dark color in the crease.
	Protruding	Keep color medium-toned, matching shadow to eye color. Try subtle fake lashes!
Eyelids	Large, Puffy	Contour the brow bone, not the crease. Keep crease lighter than brow bone.
	Small	Shape and define by using darker shades on lid and brow bone that blend together.
Lips	Full, Upper	Draw lip liner inside upper lip. Use slightly darker color than on lower lip. Gloss lower lip only.
	Full, Lower	Draw lip liner inside lower lip. Keep lip color darker than upper lip.
	Thin, Narrow: Upper and Lower	Draw lip liner outside natural lip line, and colors light and bright. Use gloss on whole mouth.
	Drooping Corners	Lift lips by drawing liner up and outward at lower corners. Pencil corners on upper lip to meet new lower lip line. Fill in with natural, medium shade lip color.
	Uneven	Fill in missing lip shape with natural color liner. Avoid glossy or greasy lipsticks that run and distort shape.

FRAGRANCE

INTERVIEWER: "What do you sleep in?"
MARILYN MONROE: "Chanel No. 5."

It seems we're "drenched" in perfume promotions these days: magazines have "scratch 'n sniff" inserts, monthly bills from department stores have scented folder strips, and there are monthly launchings of perfumes by various celebrities, with all of the media bombardment that goes with it.

The truth is, not everyone can wear certain fragrances—whether woodsy-, floral-, citrus-, or lavender-based. Body chemistry can radically change the base essence or oil from something that might smell great on your best friend to something that smells **awful** on you.

Perfume is expensive, but **cologne** and **toilet water** are less pricey, so it pays to shop wisely. Take advantage of free samples, take them home and try them at your leisure. When trying perfume in the store, spray scent into the air before you find one you like—then, spray it on the "pulse point" of your wrist. Wait for the "notes" of the fragrance to develop. The top note is what you'll smell first. It's usually sharper and smells slightly of alcohol. The middle note takes about a half hour to an hour to develop, and the bottom note, or base essence, develops after several hours. Don't test more than three perfumes a day—your sense of smell becomes confused otherwise!

To make fragrance a real part of you, use perfumed bath oil, body lotion, and shampoo, if the fragrance comes in these. Don't wear perfume while sunbathing—it discolors the skin. **Never** spray perfume or cologne or toilet water onto fine silks, linens, or wools, as it may stain the fabric.

Our sense of smell is a link to our memories, so find the fragrance that's right for you and use it every day. You'll be memorable, too!

HAIR CARE

In spite of all of the new advances in hair care products, some of us are "all thumbs" when we style our hair ourselves. Here's how to get professional results by using modern appliances and styling aids.

Gels and mousses should be applied directly to hair and spread from scalp to ends. Apply it with palms underneath, and fingertip throughout. To curl and wave, insert fingers into hair and lift roots upward while drying. After drying the scalp, dry ends while cupping the hands around them, without grabbing and squeezing. At the very end, when hair ends are still a bit damp, "scrunch" ends. Please do not use more than a golf-ball-size dollop of mousse, as you want your hair to look like hair, not like day-old cole slaw.

Blow drying can dry out hair, so use hair moisturizers to prevent damage. If you are trying to achieve a curly or natural look, you should use a diffuser. Position dryer beneath hair and dry at an angle.

Drying long hair is fast and easy if you use a high setting and blow hair dry in small sections, lifting up with a semicircular brush. Dry from roots to ends with air flow parallel to hair for a smoother look.

Give lift by bending roots with fingers with palm facing scalp. Flip hair over so palm faces up, and dry hair.

If you're right-handed, hold the hair dryer in your left hand to style your left side, and vice-versa. **Don't** reach across your face to style the opposite side.

Curling irons and crimpers can create wonderful styles in minutes, but can also dry and damage ends. Protect against split ends by using end papers. Hold the hair to be curled at a 90° angle to your head. Dry the top sections straight up, back and side sections outward, rolling hair back onto the curling iron. Keep crimper waving even on all sections for even waves all around.

Electric rollers create a lovely, soft set, which unfortunately does not last as long as the old wet set. Covered electric rollers, wide-toothed combs, and real bristle brushes won't break hair. For a quick, gentle set, spray small sections with hair spray, set with nonelectric curlers, and spray again. Comb into desired style.

Choosing the right hairstyle is very important, and a bit tricky. Just as the right makeup can flatter and improve your appearance, so can the right hairstyle. In fact, hair can affect your overall look more than makeup, because the shape of your hairdo can help or hurt your attempt to balance your figure. For example, if you have wide hips, you should not wear a hairdo that mirrors that body shape by being narrow at the top and wide on the bottom, such as a flip; nor should you exaggerate your wide bottom by wearing a tiny little gamine boy cut, unless you want to look like a pin head! Women with thick middles should not wear bowllike hairdos, and women with full bustlines should avoid "dos" that are full on top and narrow on the bottom, like the old "artichoke" do. Someone once told me that the shape of your hairdo should be the opposite of the shape of your torso, and I thought that was crazy, but, in fact, that is the truth.

Neutralizing the excesses of your body type is only one of the considerations of your ideal hairstyle. You cannot overlook **face shape**, although I think it is less important than body type, and should be considered as secondary if there is a conflict between which "divine hairdo" looks best for your figure, and which looks best for your face. In general, women with full faces should choose hairstyles with height, while women with narrow faces should opt for styles with width. Wide jaws are best softened with fullness at the top (although this trait doesn't seem to bother Christie Brinkley), while heart shapes need fullness at the bottom. Square faces look best in hairdos (and hats) that are a bit asymmetrical.

Lifestyle is another important consideration, as is **personal style**. An Olympic swimmer would be ill advised to choose a pageant bouf (that Miss America style), as her lifestyle would not allow the proper maintenance. Nor is an aspiring Miss America likely to go for a militant crew cut, as it would not be in keeping with the style and image that she is expected to project. Another important variable of lifestyle is time. How much of it do you have to fool with your tresses?

Proportion is as important in picking your hairstyle as it is in every other aspect of **Petitedom**, *i.e.*, **No Rapunzel hairdos!** A small face and frame almost always get lost under a mountain of waves. In the agency, too much **hair** was one of the two reasons most often cited for turning down a model applicant (the other: projecting too sexy an image—wholesome, fresh and clean sell on petite models, not glamorama).

If you are a working woman, choose a simple and polished hairstyle. It will not only make you look more sophisticated, but will help you to overcome that cutesy-unto-death look, which many petite women feel keeps them from being taken seriously.

Coloring Your Hair

Our friends at Glemby have some words of wisdom for us about hair coloring, gearing their advice to complement **seasonal color palettes**:

1. **Frosting or highlighting** is good for **Summers**, is very natural looking, flattering the face as it lightens and brightens. Winters, Autumns and most Springs should not frost their hair, as it will look harsh.
2. **Tints** allow you to create many different effects as you combine the colorant with your hair's own natural color, and there are a multitude of hair coloring products on the market today. You can choose either permanent (lasts longer than six weeks, then requires touch-up or reapplication) or temporary (usually washes out within six weeks, or less time if you shampoo your hair frequently) colorants. Winters and Summers should avoid reddish tints.
3. **Henna** is not recommended for fine or limp hair as it tends to weigh down the hair, and may also cause damage to the hair, although **natural** henna is easier chemically on the hair than **colored** henna products. In spite of the implications of its name, all henna does not contain red, which is only good for warm seasons. Ash-tone hennas are lovely.
4. **Rainbows (weaving)** allow you to create a "halo" effect as you go from lighter colors used on the crown to slightly darker effects as you move toward the back, with the darkest shades at the nape of the neck.
5. **Reverse frosting** is good for Winters or Autumns and involves a process that is the opposite of the "rainbow" process described above. Dark streaks are added to a lighter based hair, which is especially helpful for anyone making the transition from a "blonde" back to her natural coloring.

Hair: A Parting of the Waves

How you part your hair can make all the difference in your hairstyle, and can bring out your best facial features. Here are some tips on the art of parting, and how to find the style that's best for you:

1. A **center part** is great for oval, heart or symmetrically shaped faces, but **not** good for round or narrow faces. To pull off a center part, you must have fine, delicate, nearly perfect features, as it draws attention to any bad features you have. Also, it's been said that a center part can add years to your appearance.

2. **Side parts** can be worn by any face shape and all hair types. If your face is very narrow or round, however, try a side part that's very slightly to the side. Side parts have the added advantage of camouflaging imperfect features, too.

3. The **diagonal part** starts on one side at the back and goes forward to the opposite side at the forehead. It's really best for thick, wavy or curly hair, and bad for short, fine thin hair. Like well-cut bangs, a diagonal part can minimize a large forehead. It's a sporty, fun type of part.

Finding your natural part isn't hard. Just comb your hair straight back when it's wet and run your fingers through it once or twice—you'll see it appear.

If you've got a **widow's peak** or a **cowlick**, work with it, not against it. Part your hair at the problem; you'll also get instant lift that way.

Use mousses and spritz products to train your part and keep it neat. Parting *can* be sweet furrow!

Figure 10-5
Some classic styles for:

A. Short Hair—gamine, casual, curly

B. Medium Hair—blunt, French Bob, Cleopatra

Figure 10-5 (Continued)

C. Long Hair—pony tail, tie back, French braid

Figure 10-6

Don't forget the feminine charm and polish of hair ornaments!

There are basically three hair styles—short, medium and long. The simpler the basic cut, the more varied the dos you can create, and the better you will look, as simple is always best when it comes to hair (Figures 10-5 and 10-6).

THE AT-HOME PETITE SPA

My Aunt Maryvonne is a health spa fanatic. Not your local neighborhood variety, but the luxurious biggies like Palm-Aire, La Costa, and the Ashram. Auntie's stories of the pampering (and the pain) led me to devise an at-home petite spa that is pain-free, and leaves you relaxed and rejuvenated. Estimate about two hours for the entire spa, so make sure that you have no commitments or interruptions. Think of it as time for yourself for a change!

The night before your spa, slather your hands and feet with a super rich cream or plain petroleum jelly and slip on cotton socks and gloves. Retire earlier than usual for a deep beauty sleep.

Come morning, have a cup of herbal tea or decaffeinated coffee. Hot water into which you have squeezed the juice of a fresh lemon is also good. Keep breakfast light: a poached or boiled egg with dry toast, or some cold cereal.

A fabulous facial: Cover face and neck with baby oil. Bring a pot of water to a boil and throw in chamomile or raspberry leaves, available in health food and gourmet stores. Pour the boiling water into a large bowl and make a tent over it with a bath towel. Keep your face about seven or eight inches from the steam, taking short breaks if it feels too hot. Use a technique for easier breathing that is used in many saunas. **Breathe through clenched teeth!**

Remain over the steam for about fifteen minutes, thinking restful thoughts. When you emerge, gently wipe away the oil, then apply a masque for your specific skin type. A masque made of beaten egg white, oatmeal, and honey is good for all skin types. If blackheads are a problem, add two tablespoons of salt to the masque. Leave on for twenty to thirty minutes, then wash off with water.

A little light exercise at this point in the spa will be of benefit to both body and mind. Pop your favorite workout tape on the VCR, or play your favorite, upbeat music, while doing 30 minutes of low impact calisthenics, yoga, or stretching. You don't have to "go for the burn," but do enough to open your pores and sweat a bit.

A blissful body wrap is usually available only at expensive spas, but this is the at-home version. After your exercise session, draw a comfortably hot bath and pour in bath salts, gelée, or fragrant herbs. Soak a big towel in this water and wring out the towel. Wrap the towel around your body, and immediately wrap a plastic dropsheet over the towel. Place cotton ball dipped in witch hazel on your eyes, **after** you get on your bed. Cover the entire plastic mass with a warm blanket, and rest for fifteen minutes. A wonderful, relaxed feeling will come over you—enjoy it!

A lovely lunch.   This is my favorite part of the spa! Have a salad, some cold chicken and fruit, with a glass of seltzer with a twist of lime. Eat **leisurely**.

The end result: You'll feel cleansed and refreshed—confident that you feel and look great for whatever the day or evening has in store.

I recommend the **Petite Spa Treatment** at least twice a month—you're worth it!

POSTURE

Please Stand Up Straight!
and, if necessary,
Practice walking *gracefully*!

VOICE

If you have a grating voice or an unpleasant regional accent, seek the help of a vocal coach. Nothing ruins a pretty picture faster than an ugly sound. Further, people judge you very much on the way you speak. If grammar or vocabulary is a source of insecurity to you, take courses and/or read self-help books on the subject. Mrs. Malaprop may have been funny in literature, but no one took her seriously!

NUTRITION AND EXERCISE

Finally, it is true that "you are what you eat," and that your "body is a machine that needs to be used." For beauty, and for mental and physical health, learn all you can about *nutrition* and *exercise*. Models and other "professional beauties" are attuned to these two words. You should be, too!

11

THE PETITE YELLOW PAGES

When I started working on this book, I went to all of the usual sources for fashion trade information and found, to my utter dismay, that nothing existed for petites as a reference book. So I began what was to be the most tedious of the research for *The Complete Petite*. The result, I hope, will meet with your approval, for the last major chapter offers you something that has never been done in any fashion book, petite or otherwise. For in this chapter, you will find:

1. State-by-state listing of stores that carry petites
2. Petite catalogs for shop-by-mail fans
3. Special shopping know-how tips
4. Glossary of fashion terms
5. Fabrics and fabric care

STATE BY STATE LISTING OF STORES THAT CARRY PETITES

This chapter lists, alphabetically by state, stores that carry petite clothing. Some of these stores specialize in only petites, and some of them carry petites in addition to other things. I recommend that you call your local department stores and ask if they have petite dress and sportswear departments. Write letters to store presidents and tell them, if you are not seeing what you want and need. This makes a big difference to merchandisers, who frequently say they fell out of touch with the customers by the time they made it to the top.

Retail stores go in and out of operation all the time, so call ahead before going any distance to a new store, and watch your local paper for news of store openings.

The hardest part of assembling this list is the worry that I might leave someone out, and by so doing offend them. If such is the case, I apologize in advance.

NATIONAL CHAIN STORES
Casual Corner
J.C. Penney
K-Mart
Marshall's
Montgomery Ward
Sears and Roebuck
Walmart

NATIONAL DEPARTMENT STORES
Belk
Belk-Simpson
Bloomingdales
Dillard's
Lord & Taylor
Macy's
Marshall Field
The May Company
Neiman-Marcus
Nordstrom
Saks Fifth Avenue

MAJOR REGIONAL DEPARTMENT STORES
A & S (Abraham & Straus)
Alexanders
B. Altman
The Bon
Bonwit Teller
The Broadway
Bullock's
Burdine's
Burlington Coat Factory
Carson, Pirie, and Scott

Emporium Capwell
Famous-Barr
Filene's
Frederick and Nelson
G. Fox
Gayfer's
Glosser's
Goldwater's
Hecht's
Herberger's
Hess
Higbee's
Joseph Horne
Hunt & Peck
Hutzlers
I. Magnin
Ivey's
Jacobson's
The Jones Store
Jordan Marsh
Kaufmann's
L.S. Ayres
Lazarus
The Lion Store
Loehmanns
Maas Brothers
McAlpin's
Miller and Rhoads
Mervyn's
Meier and Frank
The Parisian
Pomeroy's
Rich's
Robinson's
Seifert's
Sibley's

Strawbridge and Clothier
Syms
Thalheimer's
John Wanamaker
Woodward and Lothrop
Yonker Bros.
ZCMI

ALABAMA

Wakefields
1212 Quintard Avenue
Anniston, AL 36202
(205) 237–9521

Parisian, Inc.
200 Research Parkway
Birmingham, AL 35211
(205) 940–4000

Rogers, Inc.
117 Court Street
Florence, AL 35631
(205) 764–8261

Five Four & Under
3015 South Memorial Parkway
Huntsville, AL 35801
(205) 880–3484

Heather's, Inc.
100 Franklin Street
Huntsville, AL 35801
(205) 533–2774

C.J. Gayfer
Springdale Plaza
Mobile, AL 36626
(205) 471–6000

Metzger's
3279 Bell Air Mall
Mobile, AL 36606
(205) 478–0417

House Next Door
2533 North Broad Street
Selma, AL 36701
(205) 872–0376

ALASKA

Nordstrom
603 "D" Street
Anchorage, AS 99501
(907) 279–7622

ARIZONA

The Broadway Southwest
4000 Fiesta Mall
Mesa, AR 85202
(602) 835–4500

Plaza Petites
Loehmann's Plaza
1837 West Guadalupe,
    Suite #106
Mesa, AR 85202
(602) 838–5677

Pint Size
84 Park Central Mall
Phoenix, AR 85013
(602) 274–5549

Plaza Petites Inc.
5625 North 19th Avenue
Phoenix, AR 85015
(602) 242–0798

Plaza Petites
Lincoln View Plaza
3151 East Lincoln Boulevard
Phoenix, AR 85016
(602) 381–1082

Susan's Petites
3431 West Thunderbird Road
Phoenix, AR 85023
(602) 863–4955

Walter Switzer, Inc.
25 East Adams Street
Phoenix, AR 85004
(602) 252–6161

Boudoir Ltd.
6166 North Scottsdale Road
Scottsdale, AR 85253
(602) 998–3782

Clara's Fashionable Boutique
10816 North Scottsdale Road
Scottsdale, AR 85254
(602) 948–0051

Oxford Scholar
6137 North Scottsdale Road
Scottsdale, AR 85253
(602) 991–4608

Robinson's
4500 North Scottsdale Road
Scottsdale, AR 85252
(602) 941–0066

Petite Fashions
10001 West Bell Road
Sun City, AR 85351
(602) 933–3914

Dillard's Southwest
1616 South Priest Drive
Tempe, AR 85281
(602) 829–5100

Eileen's of Tucson
7125 East Tanque Verde
Tucson, AR 85712
(602) 296–1517

Serendipity
P.O. Box 27500
Tucson, AR 85726–7500
(800) 972–1000

ARKANSAS

PJ's
1205 North Walton Road
Bentonville, AK 72712
(501) 273–7233

Dillard's
Sixth and Main Streets
Little Rock, AK 72203
(501) 376–5200

M.M. Cohn Co.
510 Main Street
Little Rock, AR 72203
(501) 374–3311

Martha's Missy Petite
4556 J.F. Kennedy Boulevard
North Little Rock, AK 72211
(501) 225–5588

CALIFORNIA

Hinshaw's
1201 South Baldwin Drive
Arcadia, CA 91006
(818) 446–4681

Judd's
1701 18th Street
Bakersfield, CA 93301
(805) 325–5934

Alaia Boutique
13 North Rodeo Drive
Beverly Hills, CA 90210
(213) 275–7313

J.C. Penney Co.
6131 Orangethorpe Avenue
Buena Park, CA 90624
(714) 670–2500

Prestige Petites
1875 South Bascomb Avenue
Campbell, CA 95008
(408) 559–3099

Cinderella of Boston, Inc.
P.O. Box 7110
8607 Canoga Avenue
Canoga Park, CA 91304
(818) 709–1133

Chic Petite
239 Crossroads Boulevard
Carmel, CA 93923
(408) 624–4344

Nordstrom
3333 Bristol Street
Costa Mesa, CA 92626
(714) 549–8300

Lanz of California
8680 Hayden Place
Culver City, CA 90232
(213) 558-0200

Gottschalks
860 Fulton Mall
Fresno, CA 93718
(209) 483-1111

Petites West
P.O. Box 1872
Fresno, CA 93718-1872
(209) 488-7390

Wee Women
3237 Glendale Galleria
Glendale, CA 91219
(818) 246-8000

Mervyns
25001 Industrial Boulevard
Hayward, CA 94545
(415) 785-8800

Buffums
301 Long Beach Boulevard
Long Beach, CA 90802
(213) 432-7800

Maison Petites
325 State Street
Los Altos, CA 94022
(415) 941-2779

Bona Petite
860 South Los Angeles Street
Los Angeles, CA 90014
(213) 622-0265

The Broadway
3880 North Mission Road
Los Angeles, CA 90031
(213) 227-2000

The Broadway
550 South Flower Street
Los Angeles, CA 90071
(213) 620-0150

Bullocks
800 South Hope Street
Los Angeles, CA 90017
(213) 612-5000

Bullocks Wilshire
3050 Wilshire Boulevard

Los Angeles, CA 90010
(213) 382-6161

J.W. Robinson Co.
600 West 7th Street
Los Angeles, CA 90017
(213) 488-5522

Susan's
2021 West 7th Street
Los Angeles, CA 90057
(213) 413-5127

The Petite Place
180 Leveland Lane
Modesto, CA 95350
(209) 526-0108

Bullocks
P.O. Box 91150
Pasadena, CA 91109-1150
(800) 222-9555

Gene Burton
505 South Lake Avenue
Pasadena, CA 91101
(818) 795-5821

Balisimo
1700 Catalina Avenue
Redondo Beach, CA 90277
(213) 543-5540

Lydia Petites
480 Howe Avenue
Sacramento, CA 95821
(916) 927-3848

Weinstock's
6th and 2nd Streets
Sacramento, CA 95801
(916) 449-8888

Harris's
300 North "E" Street
San Bernadino, CA 92416
(714) 889-0444

The Coat Story
The Cannery
San Francisco, CA 94133
(415) 885-6415

Emporium Capwell
835 Market Street
San Francisco, CA 94103
(415) 764-2222

Especially Petite Women
50 Post Street
San Francisco, CA 94104
(415) 781-3132

I. Magnin
135 Stockton Street
San Francisco, CA 94108
(415) 362-2100

Macy's—California
Stockton and O'Farrel Streets
San Francisco, CA 94120
(415) 397-3333

Maison Mendessalle
139 Powell Street
San Francisco, CA 94104
(415) 781-3519

Somo
59 2nd Street
San Francisco, CA 94105
(415) 777-9475

The Great American Short Story
9166 East La Rosa Drive
Temple City, CA 91780
(800) BE SHORT

Syd's Feminine Fashions
11 Del Anio Fashion Center
Torrance, CA 90503
(213) 542-9675

Chas Ford
407 Main Street
Watsonville, CA 95076
(408) 722-3341

COLORADO

Fashion Bar, Inc.
401 South Buckley Road
Aurora, CO 80017
(303) 695-7979

F.B. Petites
Boulder Crossroads Center
1600 28th Street
Boulder, CO 80301
(303) 449-8500

Chic Petite
3309 North Academy Boulevard
Colorado Springs, CO 80907
(303) 570–1510

Petite Suite
3961 Palmer Park Boulevard
Colorado Springs, CO 80909
(303) 596–0064

A Short Story
Broadmoor Hotel
Colorado Springs, CO 80901
(719) 635–1627

Thelma's Creations Ltd.
130 North Tejon Avenue
Colorado Springs, CO 80903
(303) 632–4133

F.B. Petites (Division of
Fashion Bar Department Stores)
Cherry Creek Shopping Mall
3030 East 2nd Avenue
Denver, CO 80206
(303) 321–7178

F.B. Petites
Northglenn Mall
100572 Melody Drive
Denver, CO 80233
(303) 252–0532

Perkins—Shearer
6180 East Warren Street
Denver, CO 80222
(303) 399–3277

Petite Concepts
East Bank Shopping Center
4192 South Parker Road
Denver, CO 80231
(303) 693–4229

Joslins
595 West Hampden Road
Englewood, CO 80110
(303) 762–8310

CONNECTICUT

Petites Ltd.
P.O. Box 1045
Avon, CT 06001–1045
(203) 674–1577

Skydel's
P.O. Box 2007
1050 East Main Street
Bridgeport, CT 06608
(203) 272–7640

Casual Corner Inc.
107 Phoenix Avenue
Enfield, CT 06082
(203) 741–0771

Petite Sophisticates
107 Phoenix Avenue
Enfield, CT 06082
(203) 741–3641

Silkworm
Main Street
Essex, CT 06426
(203) 767–1298

Razook's Inc.
45 East Putnam Avenue
Greenwich, CT 06830
(203) 661–6603

Jessica's Petites
Lighthouse Square, #B–3
705 Boston Post Road
Guilford, CT 06437
(203) 453–5413

G. Fox Inc.
960 Main Street
Hartford, CT 06115
(203) 552–1920

Luttegens Ltd.
1 Civic Center Plaza
Hartford, CT 06104
(203) 275–6000

Sage-Allen & Co., Inc.
900 Main Street
Hartford, CT 06103
(203) 278–2570

D + L Stores Corp.
270 John Downey Drive
New Britain, CT 06050
(203) 223–3655

Worth's
83 Bank Street
Waterbury, CT 06721
(203) 754–5101

DISTRICT OF COLUMBIA

Garfinkel's
1401 "F" Street NW
Washington, DC 20004
(202) 628–7730

MRV Beauty Salon
1010 Wisconsin Avenue NW
Washington, DC 20007
(202) 337–6324

Raleighs
1201 Connecticut Avenue NW
Washington, DC 20002
(203) 785–7000

Woodward + Lothrop
10th and "F" Streets
Washington, DC 20013
(202) 879–8000

FLORIDA

Beall's Dept. Stores Inc.
P.O. Box N
1806 38th Avenue East
Bradenton, FL 33506
(813) 747–2355

Gayfer's
P.O. Box 6340
100 Clearwater Mall
Clearwater, FL 33518
(813) 796–2341

Petite Connection
1020 East Atlantic Avenue
Delray Beach, FL 33483
(305) 977–7117

Petite Place, Inc.
453 Plaza Drive
Eustis, FL 32726
(803) 288–1063

May Florida
117 West Duval Street
Jacksonville, FL 32202
(904) 346–7311

The Vogue
6225 Powers Avenue
Jacksonville, FL 32217
(904) 737–0811

Village Petites
1907 State Road
Longwood, FL 32750
(305) 332–8086

A Nose for Clothes
8865 SW 132nd Street
Miami, FL 33176
(305) 253–8631

Burdine's
22 East Flagler Street
Miami, FL 33103
(305) 835–5151

J. Byrons Inc.
16700 NW 15th Avenue
Miami, FL 33169
(305) 620–3000

Jordon-Marsh Florida
1501 Biscayne Boulevard
Miami, FL 33121
(305) 377–1911

Oggi
1166 Kane Concourse-Bay
   Harbor
Miami, FL 33154
(305) 868–6444

Clothes Rack
539 Fifth Avenue
Naples, FL 33904
(813) 262–7489

Belk-Lindsey Co.
100 Colonial Plaza Mall
Orlando, FL 32803
(305) 894–4551

Boutique of Beauty
6016 South Orange Avenue
Orlando, FL 32890
(305) 855–6886

Frances Brewster, Inc.
P.O. Box 275
259 Worth Avenue
Palm Beach, FL 33480
(305) 655–6702

Oui Petites
559 Northwest Street
Pensacola, FL 32505
(904) 432–0661

Petite Clothiers of Seville
4400 Bayou Boulevard, #6A
Pensacola, FL 32503
(904) 476–6428

Belk-Lindsey
P.O. Box 11808
3100 First Avenue West
St. Petersburg, FL 33705
(813) 821–8211

Robinson's/Maison Blanche
66901 22nd Avenue North
St. Petersburg, FL 33710
(813) 344–4611

Eve's Petites
1465 Main Street
Sarasota, FL 34236
(813) 366–8443

Mimi's Petite Boutique
44075 Tamiami Trail
Sarasota, FL 34231
(813) 922–3384

My Petites
2065 Siesta Drive
Sarasota, FL 33579
(813) 955–0399

Colony Shops
3415 Frontage Road East
Tampa, FL 33607
(813) 877–7777

For Petites Only
13240 North Dale Mabry Drive
Tampa, FL 33618
(813) 961–0123

Maas Bros./Jordan Marsh
P.O. Box 311 (Department 38)
Franklin and Zack Streets
Tampa, FL 33601
(813) 223–7525

Maria Elena's Boutique
304 South Macdill Avenue
Tampa, FL 33609
(813) 872–6153

Wolf Bros.
2211 University Square Mall
Tampa, FL 33612
(813) 972–4448

Just Petites
140 Venice Drive
Venice, FL 22595
(813) 488–0327

The Petite Shop
3340 Ocean Drive
Vero Beach, FL 32960
(407) 231–4595

Anthony's Inc.
5000 Georgia Avenue
West Palm Beach, FL 33405
(305) 588–7336

Belk Lindsey Co.
1375 6th Street NW
Winter Haven, FL 33880
(813) 294–4251

Rheinauer's Inc.
P.O. Box 1520
Northgate Shopping Mall
Winter Haven, FL 33882–1520
(813) 294–5931

Jacobson Stores, Inc., Florida
245 Driggs Drive
Winter Park, FL 32792
(305) 677–0700

GEORGIA

Belk Department Store
2601 Dawson Road
Albany, GA 31707
(912) 436–5741

Jason's Petites
2610 Dawson Road
Albany, GA 31707
(912) 883–7757

Macy's—Atlanta
180 Peachtree Street NW
Atlanta, GA 30303
(404) 221–7221

Muse's Clothing Co.
52 Peachtree Street NW
Atlanta, GA 30303
(404) 522–5400

The Petite Place
6309 Rosewell Road, Suite 1-D
Atlanta, GA 30328
(404) 252-1223

Petites and Company
Perimeter Mall
Atlanta, GA 30346
(404) 668-0793

Rich's Inc.
P.O. Box 4539
45 Broad Street SW
Atlanta, GA 30302
(404) 586-4636

J.B. White Store
1700 Gordon Highway
Augusta, GA 30904
(404) 790-7070

Kirven's
P.O. Box 6627
Columbus Square Mall
Columbus, GA 31907
(404) 563-1311

Petite Sensations
4646 East Forsyth Road
Macon, GA 31210
(912) 477-6060

Upton's
6356 Corley Drive
Norcross, GA 30071
(404) 662-2500

Side Street of Roswell
10479 Altharetta Street
Roswell, GA 30075
(404) 998-0999

Carousel
136 Retreat Plaza
St. Simons Island, GA 31522
(912) 638-3060

Petite Friends
7400 Abercorn Street
Savannah, GA 31406
(912) 352-8841

HAWAII

Carol & Mary Ltd.
1687 Laleoukalani Boulevard
Honolulu, HA 96814
(808) 946-5075

Liberty House of Hawaii
P.O. Box 2690
1450 Ala Moana Boulevard
Honolulu, HA 96850
(808) 941-2345

Shirokiya
2250 Ala Moana Center
Honolulu, HA 96814
(808) 941-9111

Saks Boutique
8003 Kam Highway
Pearl City, HA 96782
(808) 455-5424

IDAHO

Mainstreet
2345 North Waukegan Road
Bannockburn, ID 60015
(312) 948-1600

ILLINOIS

Carson, Pririe Scott & Co.
1 South State Street
Chicago, IL 60603
(312) 744-2000

Chernin's
1001 South Clinton Street
Chicago, IL 60607
(312) 922-5900

Evans, Inc.
36 South State Street
Chicago, IL 60603
(312) 855-2000

C.J.'s Petite
203 West First Street
Dixon, IL 61021
(815) 288-7370

Complete Petite
21 South Third Street
Geneva, IL 60143
(312) 232-7979

The Little Travelers
404 South Third Street
Geneva, IL 60134
(312) 232-4200

Merra Lee Shops, Inc.
230 West State Street

Geneva, IL 60143
(312) 232-2640

Short Stop Ltd.
221 South Third Street
Geneva, IL 60134
(312) 232-7688

Bon Marche
185 South Schuyker Avenue
Kankakee, IL 60901
(815) 933-6725

B.J. Petites
318 South Main Street
Morton, IL 61550
(309) 266-5911

Brickton Ltd.
21 South Prospect Avenue
Park Ridge, ILL 60068
(312) 823-4545

The Elite Petite
106 North 6th Street
Quincy, IL 62301
(217) 222-0763

Madigan's
7440 Central Avenue
River Forest, IL 60305
(312) 771-7400

Lullaby House
3600 North Main Street
Rockford, IL 61103
(815) 877-8711

Oui Petites
Plaza DeLago
1515 Sheridan Road
Wilmette, IL 60091
(312) 356-2101

Emily Jacobi Ltd.
561-A Lincoln Avenue
Winnetka, IL 60093
(312) 446-4750

INDIANA

De Jong's Inc.
306 Main Street
Evansville, IN 47708
(812) 423-1161

Nobbson
5616 Industrial Road
Fort Wayne, IN 46825
(219) 482–8642

Rosalee Stores
P.O. Box 6288
5920 Hohman Avenue
Hammond, IN 46325
(219) 932–0156

Courtyard Cottage
2292 West 86th Street
Indianapolis, IN 46260
(317) 872–5223

Elite Petites
8727 U.S. 31 South
Indianapolis, IN 46227
(317) 887–1827

L.S. Ayres & Co.
1 West Washington Street
Indianapolis, IN 46204
(317) 262–4411

Petite Woman
6101 North Keyston
Indianapolis, IN 46220
(317) 253–3716

Ball Stores, Inc.
P.O. Box 752
Muncie, IN 47305
(317) 284–8471

Gina's Petite Shoppe
800 East McGalliard
Muncie, IN 47303
(317) 747–0766

Meis of Indiana, Inc.
2901 Ohio Boulevard
Terre Haute, IN 47803
(812) 234–5511

IOWA

Armstrong's Inc.
Third Avenue and Third Street SE
Cedar Rapids, IA 52401
(319) 363–0201

Seiferts
500 Higley Law Building
Cedar Rapids, IA 52401
(319) 364–0178

La Petite Fleur
1030 Mound Street
Davenport, IA 42801
(319) 323–3506

Peterson-Harned-Von Maur
131 West Second Street
Davenport, IA 42801
(319) 324–2641

Yonkers, Inc.
P.O. Box 1495
701 Walnut Street
Des Moines, IA 50397
(515) 244–1112

Willig's
613 Pierce Street
Sioux City, IA 51101–1271
(712) 252–1838

KANSAS

Connie's Petites
1223 Main Street
Great Bend, KS 67530
(316) 792–3000

Wolf Brothers, Inc.
P.O. Box 15905
Lenexa, KS 66215–5905
(913) 541–0018

Plaza Petites
11579 West 95th Street
Overland Park, KS 66214
(913) 541–0018

Jones Store
4000 West 71st Street
Prairie Village, KS 66208
(816) 391–7000

Scott Petites
8232 Mission Road
Prairie Village, KS 66208
(913) 642–4477

Especially Petites
8606 West 13th Street
Wichita, KS 67212
(316) 722–6264

Shepler's Inc.
6501 West Kellogg Road
Wichita, KS 67209
(316) 946–3838

KENTUCKY

C.H. Parsons Co., Inc.
P.O. Box 1508
Ashland, KY 41101–1508
(606) 325–4777

Dawahare's
1845 Alexandria Drive
Gardenside Plaza
Lexington, KY 40504
(606) 278–0422

Embry's
141 East Main Street
Lexington, KY 40507–1317
(606) 252–3461

McAlpin
2301 Richmond Road
Lexington, KY 40502
(606) 269–3611

Bacon's Department Store
3600 Bardstown Road
Louisville, KY 40218
(502) 456–4000

Behr Stores
P.O. Box 99605
1713 Cobalt Drive
Louisville, KY 40299
(502) 267–4411

Byckk's
400 Louisville Galleria
Louisville, KY 40202
(502) 582–2521

Fashion Shops of Kentucky
11008 Decimal Drive
Louisville, KY 40299
(502) 267–5415

The Petite Form
144 Chenoweth Lane
Louisville, KY 40207
(502) 895–3231

Snyder's
1740 Research Drive
Louisville, KY 40299
(502) 491–1400

Dollar General Corp.
427 Beech Street
Scottsville, KY 42164
(502) 237–5444

Dawahare's
141 Main Street
Whitesburg, KY 41858
(606) 633–4406

LOUISIANA

Weiss & Goldring
P.O. Box 1990
826 De Soto Street
Alexandria, LA 70809
(318) 443–9200

Janelle's Petites
7809 Jefferson Highway
Baton Rouge, LA 70809
(504) 928–2534

Maison Blanche/Goudchaux
1500 Main Street
Baton Rouge, LA 70801
(504) 389–7000

Abdalla's Lafayette
P.O. Box 51348
900 East St. Mary Boulevard
Lafayette, LA 70505
(318) 261–2418

Nichols Dry Goods
P.O. Box 1090
300 Sabine Street
Many, LA 71449
(318) 256–2300

D.H. Holmes Co., Ltd.
P.O. Box 60160
819 Canal Street
New Orleans, LA 70112
(504) 561–6611

Krauss Co. Ltd.
1201 Canal Street
New Orleans, LA 70112
(504) 523–3311

Beall-Ladymon
1210 Captain Shreve Drive
Shreveport, LA 71105
(318) 859–3151

Selber Brothers Inc.
P.O. Box 21830
601 Milam Street
Shreveport, LA 71120

MAINE

Intown Shop
80 Front Street
Bath, ME 04530
(207) 443–3094

Margaret Smith
Water Street
Gardner, ME 04345
(207) 582–5562

Ward Brothers, Inc.
P.O. Box 4200
72 Lisbon Street
Lewiston, ME 04240
(207) 784–7371

A.H. Benoit & Co.
Monument Square
Portland, ME 04101
(207) 773–6421

Porteous, Braun & Mitchell Co.
522 Congress Street
Portland, ME 04101
(207) 772–4681

Carroll Reed Ski Shop
510 Congress Street
Portland, ME 04101
(207) 775–7421

Howard Leather Stores
25 U.S. Highway 1
Yarmouth, ME 04096
(207) 846–5812

House of Stiles
125 Main Street
Yarmouth, ME 04520
(207) 846–4232

Shelton's
Ocean Avenue
York Beach, ME 04346
(207) 363–3810

MARYLAND

Epsteins' Department Stores
3625 East Monument Street
Baltimore, MD 21205
(301) 522–5521

Lazarus, Inc.
P.O. Box 6315
55 Baltimore Street
Cumberland, MD 21501
(301) 724–6500

Peskin's Inc.
P.O. Box 1606
145 Baltimore Street
Cumberland, MD 21502
(301) 724–0700

Jos. A. Bank Clothiers Inc.
500 Hanover Pike
Hampstead, MD 21074
(301) 239–2700

G. Briggs
611-A North Hammonds Ferry Road
Linthicum, MD 21090
(301) 636–6600

Chic Petite
12117 Rockville Pike
Rockville, MD 20852
(301) 984–0310

Hutzler's Co.
1 Joppa Road
Towson, MD 21204
(301) 825–1234

MASSACHUSETTS

Alden's Inc.
100 Ashford Street
Allston, MA 02134
(617) 787–3300

Johnny Appleseed's Inc.
50 Dodge Street
Beverly, MA 01915
(617) 922–2040

William Filene's Sons Co.
426 Washington Street
Boston, MA 02101
(617) 357–2100

Jordan Marsh Co.
450 Washington Street
Boston, MA 02205
(617) 357–3000

Talbots at Charles Square
20 University Road
Cambridge, MA 02138
(617) 576–4791

Richman-Anderson Little
P.O. Box 1660
502 Bedford Street
Fall River, MA 02722
(617) 676–1901

The Talbots
175 Beal Street
Hingham, MA 02043
(617) 749–7600

Talbots
164 North Street
Hingham, MA 02043
(800) 225–8200

Rich's Department Store
35 Congress Street
Salem, MA 01970
(617) 741–5800

CWT Specialty Stores
505 Collins Street
South Attleboro, MA 02703
(617) 399–6000

Albert Steiger Co.
1477 Main Street
Springfield, MA 01101
(413) 781–4211

Petite Connection
544 East Salem Street
Wakefield, MA 01880
(617) 246–3334

Grover Cronin Inc.
223 Moody Street
Waltham, MA 02143
(617) 894–1000

MICHIGAN

Hutzel's, Inc.
301 South Main Street
Ann Arbor, MI 48108
(313) 662–3147

Crowley Milner & Co.
2301 West Lafayette Street
Detroit, MI 48216
(313) 962–2400

Winkelman Stores Inc.
25 Parsons Street
Detroit, MI 48201
(313) 833–6900

Paradise
507 East Grand River Road
East Lansing, MI 48803
(517) 332–4299

Mr. Dino Lady Fashion
3477 Beecher Road
Flint, MI 48504
(313) 732–2611

Shorty Fashions Inc.
2907 Breton Road
Grand Rapids, MI 49508
(616) 247–1440

Paul Steketee & Sons Co.
P.O. Box 1727
86 Monroe Avenue NW
Grand Rapids, MI 49503

Jacobson Stores Inc.
1200 North West Avenue
Jackson, MI 49202
(517) 787–3600

Shorty Fashions
Maple Hill Mall
5266 West Main Street
Kalamazoo, MI 49009
(616) 455–7990

Dancer's Fashions Inc.
Box 100
566 North Cedar Road
Mason, MI 48854
(517) 676–4474

For Petite's Sake
712 Cambridge Road
Midland, MI 48640
(517) 839–0269

Alvin's Inc.
1165 Seba Road
Pontiac, MI 48054
(313) 641–1850

Town & Country
3210 Davenport Avenue
Saginaw, MI 48602
(517) 799–1490

Wiechmann's
5470 Davis Road
Saginaw, MI 48604
(517) 790–5950

MINNESOTA

Just Petites
104 West Superior Street
Duluth, MN 55802
(218) 727–8431

Marvin Oreck, Inc.
268 Southdale Shopping Center
Edina, MN 55435
(612) 927–8661

Pinstripe Petites
Southdale Center
Edina, MN 55424
(612) 925–0081

Brett's Department Stores
P.O. Box 609
1575 Mankato Mall
Mankato, MN 56002
(507) 625–6611

Dayton-Hudson Department Stores
700 Nicollet Mall
Minneapolis, MN 55402
(612) 375–2200

Donaldson's
600 Nicollet Mall
Minneapolis, MN 55402
(612) 347–7611

Jhonci's
5353 Wayzata Street
Minneapolis, MN 55402
(612) 542–9166

Pinstripe Petites
45 South 7th Street, Suite 3110
Minneapolis, MN 55402
(612) 333–0553

Pinstripe Petites
Calhoun Square
Minneapolis, MN 55408
(612) 825–1913

Salkin & Linoff, Inc.
P.O. Box 1435
7400 Excelsior Boulevard
Minneapolis, MN 55440
(612) 938–3551

VSC Inc.
215 South 11th Street
Minneapolis, MN 55403
(612) 333–4451

Wild Rose
2950 36th Avenue S.
Minneapolis, MN 55406
(612) 721–2302

Pinstripe Petites
Ridgedale Center
Minnetonka, MN 55343
(612) 545–6363

The Dahl House
P.O. Box 279
1260 West Fifth Street
Northfield, MN 55057
(507) 645–9351

Pinstripe Petites
Rosedale Center
Roseville, MN 55113
(612) 633–8677

Ehler's Apparel Inc.
415 Main Street
Red Wing, MN 55066
(612) 388–7121

Herberger's
P.O. Box H120
St. Cloud, MN 56302
(612) 251–5351

MISSISSIPPI

Waldoff's
P.O. Box 2079
999 Broadway Drive
Hattiesburg, MS 39403
(601) 544–8511

Christine's Petite Fashion
180 Highland Village
Jackson, MS 39211
(601) 366–1765

McRae's Inc.
P.O. Box 20080
3455 U.S. Highway 80 West
Jackson, MS 29309
(601) 968–4400

McAlpin's Department Store Inc.
102 South Main Street
Magee, MS 39111
(601) 849–3401

Rita's Petite
107 Ward Street
Senatobia, MS 38668
(601) 562–7602

MISSOURI

Jan's Petite Fashions
114 West 5th Street
Joplin, MO 64801
(417) 781–4933

Hall's Merchandising Inc.
200 East 25th Street
Kansas City, MO 64108
(816) 274–8231

The Jones Store
1201 Main Street
Kansas City, MO 64105
(816) 391–7000

Piccolo Petites
Crown Center
2450 Grand Avenue
Kansas City, MO 64108
(816) 274–8265

Plaza Petites
Country Club Plaza
122 Seville Square
Kansas City, MO 64105
(816) 931–2070

Swanson's
111 Nichols Road
Kansas City, MO 64112
(816) 968–6453

Helaine's Petites
320 State Street
St. Joseph, MO 49085
(816) 982–0283

The Paris
618 Felix Street
St. Joseph, MO 64501
(816) 232–8446

Dillard's
145 Crestwood Plaza
St. Louis, MO 63126
(314) 968–5890

Famous Barr Co.
601 Olive Street
St. Louis, MO 63101
(314) 444–3111

Petites Only
1340 East Battlefield
Springfield, MO 65804
(417) 882–0633

MONTANA

Hart-Albin Co.
Broadway and 2nd Avenue North
Billings, MT 59101
(406) 252–0151

NEBRASKA

J. Braggs Inc.
134 Gateway Road
Lincoln, NE 68505
(402) 467–2302

Miller & Paine
P.O. Box 81408
1229 "O" Street
Lincoln, NE 68501
(402) 474–2111

Schoenberg's, Inc.
4017 South 48th Street
Lincoln, NE 68506
(402) 489–6502

The Avenue of Omaha
616 South 75th Street
Omaha, NE 68114
(402) 391–7990

Petite Discovery
635 North 98th Street
Omaha, NE 68114
(402) 391–2959

Richman-Gordman Stores
12100 West Center Road
Omaha, NE 68144
(402) 691–4000

Zoob's
343 North 72nd Street
Omaha, NE 68114
(402) 565–2060

NEVADA

Golden Nugget Boutique
129 East Freemont Street
Las Vegas, NV 89101
(702) 385–7111

Petite Corner
5492 Meadow Wood Mall
Reno, NV 89505
(702) 323–0808

NEW HAMPSHIRE

Specially Petite
102 Plaza
76 Derry Road
Hudson, NH 03051
(603) 882–8103

Quality Shoppe
84 Main Street
Keene, NH 03040
(603) 352–0155

La Petite Boutique
Londonderry Commons
Londonderry, NH 03053
(603) 434–8048

Millers
201 Main Street
Nashua, NH 03060
(603) 882–9651

Riverside Classics
33 South Main Street
Penacook, NH 03301
(603) 753–8604

Petites of Portsmouth
19 Market Street
Portsmouth, NH 03801
(603) 431–3874

NEW JERSEY

La Petite, Inc.
401 Bloomfield Avenue
Caldwell, NJ 07006
(201) 228–8845

Flemington Furs
8 Spring Street
Flemington, NJ 08822
(201) 782–2212

Petite Cellar
211 King's Highway
Haddonfield, NJ 08033
(609) 428–2211

S.P. Dunham & Co.
Lawrence Shopping Center
Route 1 and Texas Avenue
Lawrenceville, NJ 08648
(609) 989–7777

T.J. Marche
172 Maplewood Avenue

Maplewood, NJ 07040
(201) 762–0133

NEW MEXICO

Images for Petites
1950 Juan Tabo NE
Albuquerque, NM 87112
(505) 299–7722

Linda's Fashions
8220 Menual Street NE
Albuquerque, NM 87110
(505) 298–4463

NEW YORK

Barbizon Fashion Shops
911 Central Avenue
Albany, NY 12206
(518) 489–3234

A & S
(Abraham & Straus)
20 Fulton Street
Brooklyn, NY 11201
(718) 875-7200

Adam, Melfrum & Anderson
  Co., Inc.
389 Main Street
Buffalo, NY 14205
(716) 853–4020

Gutman's
4454 Genesse Street, #23
Buffalo, NY 14225
(716) 633–2950

The Sample, Inc.
1927 Elmwood Avenue
Buffalo, NY 14207
(716) 874–1730

S.F. Izard Co. Inc.
150 North Main Street
Elmira, NY 14902
(607) 734–7171

A & S
(Abraham & Straus)
33rd St. & 6th Avenue
New York, NY 10001
(212) 594-8500

B. Altman & Co.
34th Street and Fifth Avenue

New York, NY 10016
(212) 679–7800

Bloomingdale's
1000 Third Avenue
New York, NY 10022
(212) 705–2000

Forman's
82 Orchard Street
New York, NY 10001
(212) 228–2500

Lord & Taylor
424 Fifth Avenue
New York, NY 10018
(212) 391–3344

Macy's
151 West 34th Street
New York, NY 10001
(212) 613–1000

Petite Pleasures, Inc.
1192 Madison Avenue
New York, NY 10128
(212) 369–3437

Piaffe Inc.
841 Madison Avenue
New York, NY 10021
(212) 869–3320

Saks Fifth Avenue
611 Fifth Avenue
New York, NY 10021
(212) 753–4000

Short 'N Sweet Boutique
173 Merrick Road
Oceanside, NY 11572
(516) 766–2049

B. Forman Co.
Midtown Plaza
Rochester, NY 14604
(716) 325–6000

McCrudy & Co.
Midtown Plaza
Rochester, NY 14604
(716) 232–1000

Sibley, Lindsay & Carr Co.
228 East Main Street
Rochester, NY 14604
(716) 423–2000

The Carl Co.
430 East State Street
Schenectady, NY 12305
(518) 374–9111

Chappell's
Northern Lights Mall
Syracuse, NY 13212
(315) 455–5661/5711

Dey's
P.O. Box 1198
401 South Salina Street
Syracuse, NY 13201
(315) 474–2711

Saks Fifth Avenue
557 Tuckahoe Road
Yonkers, NY 10710
(800) 345–3454

NORTH CAROLINA

Belk Yates Co.
P.O. Box 100
Asheboro, NC 27203
(919) 629–9161

Belk Department Store
5 South Tunnel Road
Asheville, NC 28805
(704) 298–4970

Marine Corps Exchange 0131
Building 895
Camp Lejeune, NC 28542
(919) 451–2481

Belk Brothers Co.
P.O. Box 31660
Charlotte, NC 28231–1660
(704) 377–4251

Ivey's
P.O. Box 34799
127 North Tryon Street
Charlotte, NC 28234
(704) 372–3511

Petite Panache
1041 Providence Road
Charlotte, NC 28207
(704) 334–5833

Exclusively Petites
Westwood Village/SC
Clemmons, NC 27012
(919) 766–4663

Belk-Hensdale
P.O. Box 1029
4525 Camp Ground Road
Fayetteville, NC 28302
(919) 864–3211

Little Women
500H East Cornwallis Drive
Greensboro, NC 27405
(919) 378–0322

Petite Image
2157 North Center Street
Hickory, NC 28601
(704) 324–1648

Spainhour's
P.O. Box 609
246 Union Square
Hickory, NC 28601
(704) 322–5380

National of Lexington
P.O. Box 1002
400 National Boulevard
Lexington, NC 27292–1002
(704) 249–6841

Lazarus Inc.
110 North Green Street
Morgantown, NC 28655
(704) 437–4341

Christian's
P.O. Box 20441
North Hills Mall
Raleigh, NC 27609
(919) 787–8389

Le Montage Ltd.
1637 North Market Drive
Raleigh, NC 27609
(919) 876–5500

Hudson-Belk Co.
P.O. Box 111
319 Fayetteville Street
Raleigh, NC 27602
(919) 782–7010

Tyler House
304 Glenwood Avenue
Raleigh, NC 27603
(919) 834–7701

Baldwin's
P.O. Box 1868
Rocky Mount, NC 27801–1868
(919) 443–4156

Belk Tyler
1100 North Wesleyan Boulevard
Rocky Mount, NC 27804
(919) 977–2355

Spainhour's
P.O. Box 1187
1647 East Broad Street
Statesville, NC 28677
(704) 872–6335

Belk Berry Co.
P.O. Box 4369
3500 Oleander Drive
Wilmington, NC 28403
(919) 392–1440

H.L.S. Petites
315 North Front Street
Wilmington, NC 28401
(919) 251–1515

OHIO

The M. O'Neil Co.
226 South Main Street
Akron, OH 44308
(216) 375–5000

Petites by Tangerine, Inc.
1702 Merriman Road
Akron, OH 44313
(216) 867–1280

Carlisle's
P.O. Box 692
5409 Main Avenue
Ashtabula, OH 44004
(216) 997–5111

The Petite Shop
24111 Chagrin Boulevard
Beachwood, OH 44122
(216) 831–1128

Fred W. Uhlam & Co.
P.O. Box 709
126 North Main Street
Bowling Green, OH 43402
(419) 252–7505

Stern & Mann
Box 446 Downtown Station
300 2nd Street
Canton, OH 44702
(216) 455–0221

Henri's Dress Shop
5213 Glenway Avenue
Cincinnati, OH 45238
(513) 251–5213

Lazarus
7th and Race Streets
Cincinnati, OH 45202
(513) 379–7000

McAlpin's
13 West Fourth Street
Cincinnati, OH 45202
(513) 352–4400

The Higbee Co.
100 Public Square
Cleveland, OH 44113
(216) 579–2580

Kelly Kitt
689 South Green Road
Cleveland, OH 44121
(216) 292–2359

The May Co.
158 Euclid Avenue
Cleveland, OH 44114
(216) 664–6000

Madison's
72 North High Street
Columbus, OH 43215
(614) 221–4325

Petite Lady
1877 West Henderson Road
Columbus, OH 43220
(614) 451–1184

Elder-Berman Stores
P.O. Box 1448
3155 El-Bee Road
Dayton, OH 45439
(513) 296–2700

Denmark Fur Shop
322 Market Street
Steubenville, OH 43952
(614) 282–4503

The Lion Store
300 Southwick Mall
Toledo, OH 43614
(419) 535–9500

OKLAHOMA

Balliet's, Inc.
50 Penn Place
Oklahoma City, OK 73118
(405) 848–7811

Chiarelli's Petites
11940 North May Avenue
Oklahoma City, OK 73120
(405) 755–4960

Rothchild's
8100 North Classen Boulevard,
    Suite 101
Oklahoma City, OK 73114
(405) 840–3661

Streets
201 Northeast 50th Street
Oklahoma City, OK 73105
(405) 524–3322

Peggy's Petites
8212 East 71st Street
Tulsa, OK 74133
(918) 252–9464

Renberg's
311 South Main Street
Tulsa, OK 74103
(918) 585–5601

OREGON

Emporium
P.O. Box 5467
86776 McVay Highway
Eugene, OR 97405
(503) 746–9611

Kaufman's
P.O. Box 689
135 West Broadway
Eugene, OR 97440
(503) 485–1581

Peggy's Petites
1438 West Park Plaza
Ontario, OR 97914
(503) 889–3325

Just Petites
Clackamas Town Center
12000 Southwest 82nd Avenue
Portland, OR 97266
(503) 659–2246

Meier & Frank
621 Southwest Fifth Avenue
Portland, OR 97204
(502) 223–0512

Nordstrom
701 Southwest Broadway
Portland, OR 97205
(503) 224–6666

The Petite Woman's Shoppe
Water Tower Building
5331 Southwest Macadam Avenue
Portland, OR 97201
(503) 241–8595

PENNSYLVANIA

Hess Department Stores
Hamilton Mall
9th Street
Allentown, PA 18101
(215) 821–3477

H. Lehr & Co.
626 Hamilton Mall
Allentown, PA 18101
(215) 434–5181

The Petite Shop
1871 South Fifth Street
Allentown, PA 18103
(215) 791–3131

The Dry Goods, Inc.
200 Turner Industrial Way
Aston, PA 19014
(215) 497–4400

Donecker's
409 North State Street
Ephrata, PA 17522
(717) 733–2231

Pomeroy's Inc.
P.O. Box 1867
Fourth and Market Streets
Harrisburg, PA 17105
(717) 238–1661

Glosser Bros.
112 Franklin Street
Johnstown, PA 15901
(814) 536–6633

Watt & Shand
P.O. Box 3300
2 East King Street
Lancaster, PA 17603
(717) 397–5221

Danks & Co.
152 East Market Street
Lewistown, PA 17044
(717) 248–6794

Hart's
955 Fourth Avenue
New Kensington, PA 15068
(412) 337–6504

John Wanamaker
1300 Market Street
Philadelphia, PA 19101
(215) 422–2000

La Petite Femme
9337 Krewstown Road
Philadelphia, PA 19115
(215) 969–4501

Piaffe
1700 Sansom Street
Philadelphia, PA 19103
(215) 972–1547

Strawbridge & Clothier
801 Market Street
Philadelphia, PA 19105
(215) 629–6000

Accent on Petites
Station Square
Pittsburgh, PA 15219
(412) 261–0699

Joseph Horne Co.
501 Penn Avenue
Pittsburgh, PA 15222
(412) 553–8000

Kaufmann's
400 Fifth Avenue
Pittsburgh, PA 15219
(412) 232–2000

Boscov's Department Stores
4500 Perkiomen Avenue
Reading, PA 10606
(215) 779–2000

The Globe Store
119 Wyoming Avenue
Scranton, PA 18501
(717) 344–7271

S. Grubacher & Son
2801 East Market Street
York, PA 17403
(717) 757–7660

Mailman's Department Stores
Queensgate Shopping Center
York, PA 17403
(717) 845–3521

SOUTH CAROLINA

Gallant-Belk Co.
2101 North Main Street
Anderson, SC 29621
(803) 225–2511

Kerrison's
260 King Street
Charleston, SC 29401
(803) 722–4401

Belks of Columbia
P.O. Box 1497
Columbia Mall, SC 29202–1497
(803) 788–7830

James L. Tapp Co.
P.O. Box 247
1644 Main Street
Columbia, SC 29202
(803) 765–2411

Garrett's Inc.
805 By-Pass 123
Easley, SC 29640
(803) 859–1865

Belk-Simpson
P.O. Box 528
Haywood Mall
Greenville, SC 29602
(803) 297–3200

Petite Collections
1102 Woods Crossing Road

Greenville, SC 29607
(803) 288–1063

Belk
P.O. Drawer 3909
Myrtle Beach, SC 29578–3909
(803) 448–1516

Little Women
Briarcliff Mall
Myrtle Beach, SC 29578–3909
(803) 272-2088

Petite Designs
2501 Myrtle Square Mall
Myrtle Beach, SC 29577
(803) 626–8636

Marine Corps Exchange 0161
Marine Corps Recruit Depot
Parris Island, SC 29905
(803) 525–3301

Belk-Hudson Co.
P.O. Box 5787
Spartenburg, SC 29301–5787
(803) 574–1660

SOUTH DAKOTA

Michael's
314 South Main Avenue
Sioux Falls, SD 57102
(605) 339–1150

TENNESSEE

Proffit's Inc.
P.O. Box 388
Midland Center
Alcoa, TN 36691
(615) 983–7000

Goody's
P.O. Box 746
1612 Congress Parkway
Athens, TN 37303
(615) 745–5280

C. Ann's Petites
330 Franklin Road
Brentwood, TN 37027
(615) 371–8280

The Leader
511 Market Street
Chattanooga, TN 37402
(615) 266–0707

Loveman's Inc.
800 Market Street
Chattanooga, TN 37402
(615) 265–3511

C. Ann's Petites
7240 Kingston Pike
Knoxville, TN 37919
(615) 584–8116

Ira A. Watson Co.
P.O. Box 22900
200 Hayfield Road
Knoxville, TN 37933
(615) 690–6000

Rickie's Petites
5111 Homberg Drive
Knoxville, TN 37919
(615) 584–2668

Designer Petites
4556 Poplar Street
Laurelwood, TN 38117
(901) 767–7177

Goldsmith's
123 South Main Street
Memphis, TN 38103
(901) 766–2323

Helen of Memphis
1808 Union Avenue
Memphis, TN 38104
(901) 274–0867

Petites for Less
6510 Winchester Avenue
Memphis, TN 38115
(901) 794–3371

Petite MS
65-10 Winchester
Memphis, TN 38115
(901) 366–5191

Gus Mayer
2159 Green Hills Mall
Nashville, TN 37215
(615) 383–4771

The Castner Knott Good Co.
618 Church Street
Nashville, TN 37219
(615) 256–6411

McClure's Department Store
Harpeth Plaza Highway 100
Nashville, TN 37205
(615) 356–8822

TEXAS

Cinderella Petites
2401 South Street
Abilene, TX 79605
(915) 676–8490

Scarborough's
P.O. Box 849
2901 Capitol of Texas Highway
Austin, TX 78767
(512) 327–6000

The Fair Inc.
P.O. Box 4047
Beaumont, TX 77704–4047
(409) 892–6010

The White House
154 Atagg Drive
Beaumont, TX 77701
(409) 838–6131

Army and Air Force Exchange
3911 South Walton Walker
   Boulevard
Dallas, TX 75222
(214) 780–2011

Elite Petite
11441 Stemmons Freeway,
   Suite 233
Dallas, TX 75229
(214) 241–7307

Neiman-Marcus
Main and Ervay Streets
Dallas, TX 65201
(214) 741–6911

Schwab, Taylor & Gavender
P.O. Box 585049
Dallas, TX 75258
(214) 638–7762

Dillard's Department Stores
4501 North Beach Street
Fort Worth, TX 76111
(817) 831–5111

Dunlap Co.
200 Greenleaf Street

Fort Worth, TX 76107
(817) 336–4985

Monnig's
P.O. Box 2200
Fort Worth, TX 76113–2200
(817) 332–7211

Petites Ltd.
5362 West Vickery Boulevard
Fort Worth, TX 76107
(817) 731–1022

Stripling & Cox
6370 Camp Bowie Boulevard
Fort Worth, TX 76116
(817) 738–7361

Craig's
5631 Braxton Boulevard
Houston, TX 77036
(713) 780–4883

Foley's
P.O. Box 1971
1110 Main Street
Houston, TX 77251
(713) 651–7038

Palais Royal
P.O. Box 35167
10201 South Main Street
Houston, TX 77235
(713) 667–5601

Hachar Department Store
P.O. Box 1579
1119 Farragut Street
Laredo, TX 78040
(512) 723–9141

Malouf's
8201 Quaker Avenue
Lubbock, TX 79424
(806) 794–9500

Lady Odessa
4007 Parkway
Odessa, TX 79762
(915) 362–8888

Dillard's Department Stores
P.O. Box 17040
9315 Broadway
San Antonio, TX 78217
(512) 821–7611

Frost Bros.
217 East Houston Street
San Antonio, TX 78205
(512) 226–7131

La Feria Department Stores
4062 Commerce Street
San Antonio, TX 78285
(512) 223–5566

Scrivner's
8502 Broadway
San Antonio, TX 78217
(512) 824–2353

Solo Serve Corp.
3200 East Houston Street
San Antonio, TX 78219
(512) 225–7163

UTAH

Nordstroms of Salt Lake City
50 South Main Street
Salt Lake City, UT 84144
(801) 322–4200

Z.C.M.I.
2200 South (Opp. West Street)
Salt Lake City, UT 84137
(801) 321–6179

VERMONT

Little Women
1 Town Market Place
Essex, VT 05452
(802) 879–9465

Carroll Reed
Equinox Square
Manchester, VT 05462
(802) 362–3253

VIRGINIA

Hecht's
685 North Gleve Road
Arlington, VA 22203
(703) 558-1200

Leggett Department Stores
P.O. Box 5149
5200 West Mercury Boulevard
Hampton, VA 23605
(804) 827–8100

Main's Smart Shop
2220 Kecoughton Road
Hampton, VA 23661
(804) 244–2395

Globman's
P.O. Box 711
115 East Church Street
Martinsville, VA 24112
(703) 632–3404

T.H. Mandy
P.O. Box 1685
2930 Prosperity Avenue
Merrifield, VA 22116
(703) 698–8909

Leggett's
P.O. Box 12752
Military Circle Shopping Center
Norfolk, VA 23510
(804) 461–3504

Smith & Welton Inc.
300 Granby Street
Norfolk, VA 23510
(804) 640–2000

Petite Place
Tanglewood Mall
Roanoke, VA 24013
(703) 774–0087

Petite Place
Valley View Mall
Roanoke, VA 24013
(703) 362–1322

Miller & Rhoads
517 East Broad Street
Richmond, VA 23219
(804) 648–3111

Petite Editions
Chesterfield Mall
Richmond, VA 23220
(804) 379–2319

Sternheimer's
P.O. Box 26926
Richmond, VA 23261
(804) 226–1324

Thalhimer Bros.
P.O. Box 26788
615 East Broad Street
Richmond, VA 23261
(804) 643–4211

S.H. Heironimus Co.
P.O. Box 1580
405 South Jefferson Street
Roanoke, VA 24007
(703) 343–6941

WASHINGTON

Lipman's
401 Park Place, Suite 325
Kirkland, WA 98033
(206) 827–5444

The Bon
Third and Pine Streets
Seattle, WA 98181
(206) 344–2121

Frederick & Nelson
Fifth Avenue and Pine Street
Seattle, WA 98111
(206) 682–5500

Nordstrom, Inc.
P.O. Box 870
1501 Fifth Avenue
Seattle, WA 98101
(206) 628–2111

Nordstrom
100 Southcenter Shopping Center
Seattle, WA 98818
(206) 364–8800

Nordstrom Place Two
4315 University Way NE
Seattle, WA 98052
(206) 632–9516

The Crescent
P.O. Box 1515
710 West Riverside Avenue
Spokane, WA 99210
(509) 838–3311

WEST VIRGINIA

Charleston Department Stores, Inc.
1661 West Washington Street
Charleston, WV 25312
(304) 346–6793

Stone & Thomas
P.O. Box 1673
Lee and Dickinson Streets
Charleston, WV 25326
(304) 346–0981

Dils Bros. & Co., Inc.
P.O. Box 1467 (Department 2)
521 Market Street
Parkersburg, WV 26102
(304) 422–3521

Carter Nelson Ladies' Apparel
855 Mercer Street
Princeton, WV 24740
(304) 425–2677

Stone & Thomas
1030 Main Street
Wheeling, WV 26003
(304) 232–3344

WISCONSIN

Kohl's Department Stores
2315 North 124th Street
Brookefield, WC 53226
(414) 784–4480

H.C. Prange Co.
P.O. Box 19080
301 North Washington Street
Green Bay, WC 54307
(414) 435–6611

Yost's
201 State Street
Madison, WC 53703
(608) 257–2545

P.A. Bergner & Co.
331 West Wisconsin Avenue
Milwaukee, WC 53202
(414) 347–4141

Brill's
P.O. Box 17769
5900 North Port Washington Road
Milwaukee, WC 53217
(414) 964–4414

I'm Petite
8843 West North Avenue
Milwaukee, WC 53226
(414) 453–6620

PETITE CATALOGS FOR
SHOP-BY-MAIL FANS

With more than 50% of American women now in the workforce, leisurely shopping is no longer the pastime of many women whose mothers and grandmothers kept the department stores busy, Monday to Friday, while their husbands were away earning the family living. As a result, each year, more women are joining the ranks of the Shop-by-Mail devotees. Further lack of time for pleasant strolls through the local "Dream Emporiums" no doubt accounts for the latest trend, TV shopping. Some of the TV home shopping companies are now showing clothing in petites, and there are many catalogs designed for us.

Almost all major department and chain stores now carry petites—don't overlook their stores and catalogs.

There are two catalogs, which are quite extensive, and exclusively for petites:

J.C. Penney Catalog, Petites #TA 953–2284 A
P.O. Box 0370
Milwaukee, WI 53263–0370

"Proportion," Speigel Petite Catalog
P.O. Box 6340
Chicago, ILL 60680–6340

Specialty Store/Mail Order Catalogs

Write or call as indicated for catalog.

Appleseeds Collection
Department 1590
50 Dodge Street
Beverly, MA 01915

The Chelsea Collection
340 Poplar Street
Hanover, PA 17333

Pickwick Plaza
Department E3
20 Jerusalem Avenue, Suite 393
Hicksville, NY 11801

The Jones Store
1201 Main Street
Kansas City, MO 64105

Lanz Dress Catalogue
Call toll-free: 1–800–356–1271

Hall of Hanover
340 Poplar Street
Hanover, PA 17333

Old Pueblo Traders   *Send $1.00*
Department EERI
3740 East 34th Street
Tuscon, AR 85713

Petite MS
65-10 Winchester Road
Memphis, TN 38115

Serendipity
Department ADC 4
3740 East 34th Street
Tucson, AR 85713

Strictly Petites
500 East Main Street
Kilgore, TX 75662

The Tog Shop
516 Lester Square
Americus, GA 31710

Land's End
Land's End Lane
Dodgeville, WI 53595–0001

Carroll Reed
Mail Order Department
Conway, NH 03866

Avon Fashions, Inc.
Avon Lane
Newport News, VA 23630–1124

Blair
Warren, PA 13666

Royal Silk
79 Fifth Avenue
New York, NY 10003

Premiere Editions
340 Poplar Street
Hanover, PA 17333

Barrie-Pace Direct Route
921 Eastwind Drive, Suite 114
Westville, OH 43081

The Talbots
164 North Street
Hingham, MA 02043

Eurica Designers
P.O. Box 590205
San Francisco, CA 94159

Bloomingdale's by Mail
Department 445
P.O. Box 4260
Huntington Station, NY 11746–4260

SFA (Saks Fifth Avenue) Collections*
557 Tuckahoe Road
Yonkers, NY 10710

*Also ask for Anne Klein II
Petites at this address.

Marshall-Field & Co.
"Measure for Measure" Petite Catalog
111 North State Street
Chicago, IL 60690

Garfinkels' Catalog Division
9700 Philadelphia Court
Lanham, MA 20706

Dillard's Catalog Division
P.O. Box 7123
Fort Worth, TX 76111–0123

I. Magnin   *$6.00 per year*
2001 Broadway
Oakland, CA 94612

Neiman-Marcus   *$5.00 per year*
Box 2968
Dallas, TX 75221–9950

Macy's   *$3.00 per year*
Advertising Service Department
151 West 34th Street
New York, NY 10001

Bullock's Wilshire
Catalog Division
Metro Station, P.O. Box 55029
Los Angeles, CA 90955–5029

Nordstrom's
15051 Fifth Avenue
Seattle, WA 98101

J.W. Robinson's
"Club 5'4'"" Catalog Division
600 West Seventh Street
Los Angeles, CA 90017

Petite and Hard-to-Fit Shoe Catalogs

Cartain's Classic
1201 West Magnolia Avenue
Fort Worth, TX 76104

Chernin's
1001 South Clinton Street
Chicago, IL 60607

Giordano's
1118 1st Avenue
New York, NY 10021

Footsaver   *Send $1.00*
38 West 34th Street
New York, NY 10001

Elite Petite Shoes
11441 Stemmons Freeway
Dallas, TX 75247

Lawson and Marcia Hill
816 Commerce Street
Lynchburg, VA 24504

Selby Fifth Avenue
417 Fifth Avenue
New York, NY 10016

Cinderella of Boston
Department GS–88
8607 Canaoga Avenue
P.O. Box 7110
Canaoga Park, CA 91304

Wide World of Comfort
P.O. Box 511
Lafayette Hill, PA 19444

Cosmapedics
340 Poplar Street
Hanover, PA 17333

Hosiery

Socks Galore and More
P.O. Box 1515
Franklin, TX 37064

Hats

Worth and Worth Ltd.
331 Madison Avenue (at 43rd Street)
New York, NY 10017

Custom Patternmakers

Computer-made patterns made from
your basic measurements:

Clothing Design Concepts
Kansas City, MO
Call for information: 1–800–348–7255

Maternity Catalogs

There is very little petite maternity wear.
Here are some places where you can order
by mail.

Pro Creations—Leasewear
P.O. Box 22253
Portland, OR 97222–2253

Page Boy
8918 Govenor's Row
Dallas, TX 75247

Re-Creations
Department G488
P.O. Box 091038
Columbus, Ohio 43209–1038

Reborn Maternity   *Send $2.00*
564 Columbus Avenue
New York, NY 10024

Motherhood
1330 Colorado Avenue
Santa Monica, CA 90401–3381

Mom's the Word
2415 San Ramon Valley Boulevard
San Ramon, CA 94583

SPECIAL SHOPPING KNOW-HOW TIPS

Shopping Tips

To buy or not to buy—that is the question. And the shopper's ultimate moment of truth. Here's an easy checklist to help you arrive at your final decision. Give each garment or accessory one plus or one minus point for each category.

	Plus		Minus	
Form	Slimming	_____	Fattening	_____
Line	Elongating	_____	Widening	_____
Texture	Matte or soft	_____	Thick or nubby	_____
Personality	It's me	_____	Not me	_____
Lifestyle	I'll wear it often	_____	Maybe I'll wear it	_____
Scale	Trim	_____	Oversized	_____
Fit	Perfect	_____	Needs alterations	_____
Drape	Fluid	_____	Stiff	_____
Color	Flattering	_____	Just OK, or worse	_____
TOTAL	+ _____		− _____	Score: _____

7 points or more   It's a great garment—buy it!

5–6 points   It's acceptable, but won't be a favorite

4 points or less   Forget it!

Quality Tips

The following checklist will be invaluable in comparing price to quality. Consider these points carefully:

Condition

   1. Can you spot any imperfection?
   2. Does the material feel good against the skin?
   3. When you crush it briefly in your hand, do wrinkles smooth out easily?
   4. Is the color even?

Assembly

   1. Do patterns match at construction points and move in the same direction?

2. Is the garment well constructed? Seams should be sewn evenly, with even stitch tension and marked thread color. Seam allowances should be of good size and lie flat. Hems should have good fabric allowance.
3. Collars should have good shape and "roll."
4. Trims, buttons, zippers, and fasteners as well as other ornamentation should be well placed or attached. Buttonholes should not be frayed, too tight, or stretched out. If there are shoulder pads, they should be flattering, of good quality, and set into the shoulder line correctly.

Care Instructions—As a $$$ Consideration

By law all garments must have correct care labels sewn in. Consider the time you have to spend and how you prefer to maintain your wardrobe before making your purchase.

Quick Shopping Tips

If you dislike dressing rooms and "hit-or-miss" try-ons, here's a simple tip. Always shop with a tape measure on hand so that you can measure garments. This frees you from waiting in line for a dressing room, and allows you to cover a large part of the department quickly. Here's how:

1. Know your basic measurements, including your arm length and leg inseam measurements.
2. If the flat measurement of the garment is at least 3″ larger than you are at the bust or hip and ½″ larger in the waist, the item will fit 99% of the time.

Discount Shopping

Off-price and designer outlets can save you 20% to 70% on the delectable items you covet.

We often rely on word-of-mouth wholesale havens from friends and other strangers—here are two wonderful books of nationwide listings of outlets, warehouses, and wholesale stores to help you shop coast-to-coast.

1. *S.O.S.—The Save on Shopping Directory*, by Sue Goldstein (Warner Books, $10.95)
2. *The Shoppers Guide to Off Price Shopping*, by Iris Ellis (Villard Books, $4.50)

There's also a newsletter to keep you *au-courant* with new store launchings:

"SOS—Fabulous Finds"
9109 San Jose Boulevard
Jacksonville, Florida 32217

Special Clothes for Special Petites

Arthritis, disease, and physical handicaps that mean confinement to bed, wheelchair, or walker make dressing difficult and frustrating. Here's quick help in making that part of your life easier:

1. Look for jackets and tops that are easily put on, such as those that are buttonless or oversized. Dropped, large-cut armholes with raglan or dolman sleeves are good choices. Avoid garments with back button closures—they're hard enough for "able" people to manage!

2. Skirts are best in wraparound styles. Pants should have easy side entrances. If there are elastic waistbands on bottoms, they should fit comfortably. Pockets are great for stashing items—just make sure pocket depth is deep enough.

3. Cut off buttons and sew up the buttonholes. Resew buttons over the closed holes and substitute velcro tabs as fasteners, and you will be able to slip into and out of garments easily. Zippers should have good-sized rings attached.

4. If you sew at home, use electric scissors and hat or quilt pins, along with a sewing machine, to make work fast and easy.

5. Many accessories, such as collars, bows, and hair ornaments, come pre-tied and ready-to-wear.

6. Jewelry should be easy to slip on: long necklaces and chains, bracelets with expandable openings, and clip earrings make life much easier.

To make shopping easier, write for these catalogs that feature fashionable clothing for the motion-impaired:

Rolling Thunder
1128 Nuuane Avenue, Suite #100
Honolulu, HI 96817

Comfortably Yours
52 Hunter Avenue
Maywood, NJ 07607

G. Street Fabric
Mail Order Department
11854 Rockville Pike
Rockville, MD 20852

Irwin-Taylor Facile Fashions
P.O. Box 10510
Rochester, NY 14610

GLOSSARY OF FASHION TERMS

ACRYLIC: A man-made fabric that is durable, strong, inexpensive and which has good draping ability. It is exceptionally lightweight.

A-LINE: A garment that is shaped gradually away from the body, flared effectively, from top to bottom.

ANALOGOUS: Related colors sharing a common hue. They are situated closely on the color wheel, such as orange and purple, which are analogous colors of red.

ART DECO: An innovative design and architectural style developed during the early part of the 20th century, noted for its angular, rectangular shapes.

ARGYLE: Diamond-shaped design of different colors, where the diamond areas are formed with their own complete stitches.

ASCOT: A broad neck scarf on a blouse, which can be tied in a variety of ways. The ascot is a unisex accessory.

AVANT-GARDE: Unconventional, original designs, which often lead the way in fashion and set trends.

AVIATOR JACKET (also called a "bomber" jacket): Usually cut in leather, and of a design originally used by aviators. It is a blouson style *jacket*.

AWNING STRIPES: An evenly striped pattern used on decorative awnings seen at shops, hotels, and restaurants. They are also used in shirts and in dresses, usually in cotton.

BAROQUE PEARLS: Pearls irregular in form, and of medium to medium-large size.

BATIK: A popular method of dyeing fabric, done extensively with fabrics from Indonesian/Asian countries. Wax is applied in a pattern to fabric; the wax cracks during the dyeing process and creates a webbed, veiny effect in the fabric.

BATWING: Extremely full-cut sleeves that extend from the waist to the wrist.

BELLOWS POCKET: Originally part of a military uniform, a bellows pocket features an inverted pleat and a button. (The pocket was used by soldiers to store their ammunition.)

BLEND: A fabric that is a combination of two, three, or more fibers, each of which is used to give certain characteristics to the finished product.

BLOUSON: A loose jacket or blouse having a gathered bottom at the waist (can be either a set-in waist or a drawstring), or a loose blouse, which has been tucked in after the arms are raised then lowered.

BOXED PLEATS: Pleats that appear box-shaped whether pressed or unpressed.

BROADCLOTH: A plain-weave fabric in silk, cotton, wool, or synthetics with a fine-finish. This simple back and forth weave is a classic.

BROCADE: A rich, heavy fabric with intricate raised designs woven into it.

BUSTIER: Very similar in shape and styling to a camisole, but structured to simulate the stays and fittings used years ago in making corsets.

CABBAGE ROSE: A rose pattern in which the roses are large and "full-blown" in appearance.

CAMISOLE: A bare sliplike top with thin straps, which is cut straight across the bustline.

CAMP SHIRT: A boxy short-sleeved shirt, usually made of cotton in prints or solids.

CHALLIS: Lightweight twill, which is often in a printed paisley design. Twill refers to fabric with a fine, one-directional rib.

CHARMEUSE: A satin fabric of medium weight. Charmeuse can be softly draped, and has a high luster. Jean Harlow wore a lot of bias-cut (cut on the diagonal) charmeuse.

CHEMISE: Simply an unbelted dress cut in a straight line. This style works well in many different fabrics.

CHIFFON: A plainly woven sheer fabric, very soft and lightweight— chiffon is floaty and feminine.

CLUTCH: Small purse, usually hand held, *i.e.*, clutched.

COMPLEMENTARY COLORS: Any two colors (or hues) in the spectrum, which are situated directly opposite each other on the color wheel. Combined in equal amounts, complementary colors will make gray.

CORDUROY: Durable, velvetlike cotton or rayon fabric with wide or narrow cords.

COWLED BODICE: Fullness extending across the bodice from the shoulder seam to shoulder; very drapey.

CREPE: Crinkled, closely woven, thin fabric, which is opaque, yet amazingly light, and therefore wonderful for elegant daytime or evening apparel.

CREPE DE CHINE: The surface of this fabric is very similar to crepe in appearance. It is usually made of silk jersey, and often made in polyester or poly blend.

CROP TOP: Short (sometimes boxy) top that bares the midriff.

DENTED PEARLS: Irregularly shaped pearls.

DHOTI PANTS: Billowy pants (originating in India) or trousers styled with fabric blousing from the waist between the legs to the knees.

DIRNDL SKIRT: Simple, plain skirt style, which falls in a straight, narrow line from a slightly gathered waistband.

DOBBY PRINT: A Jacquard-like solid fabric with a design woven into the pattern.

DOLMAN SLEEVE: Sort of a "modified batwing" sleeve. Dolman styling is an armhole cut halfway to the waist. It is the large armhole itself that allows the upper sleeve to have such volume, which, in turn, tapers to a fitted wrist.

DROP SHOULDER: Shoulder sleeve styling where the seam is dropped below the shoulder level.

DUSTER: Long, swingy, oversized coat, usually cut in a lightweight fabric.

EPAULET: Originally used on military uniforms as a decorative shoulder strap or piece.

EVENING COLUMN: Narrow shift or sheath, floor-length and body-skimming.

FAILLE: A fabric often manufactured in silk, woven to have a fine rib (or ridge).

FEDORA: A man-tailored felt hat with a creased crown and a small-to-medium size brim.

FLANGE: An extended shoulder, which usually gives a broadened effect.

FLANNEL: Soft, plain fabric with a slightly napped surface; usually in a twill weave.

FORM-FITTING Semi-fitted or bias-cut styles that give a fitted definition to the feminine silhouette, but are not clingy or full.

FOULARD: Fabric pattern or weave made up of a small repeating geometric pattern, originally used for men's silk necktie designs.

GABARDINE: Durable, tightly woven fabric made from a twisted yarn that has a fine, diagonal effect on one side.

GAUZE: A very light, sheer, open weave fabric, very plainly woven in an open crisscross fashion.

GLEN PLAID: A simple scot plaid usually used for suits or skirts.

HABERDASHERY STYLES: Tailored menswear styles.

HANDKERCHIEF LINEN: The finest, softest, and most lightweight linen.

HAREM PANTS: Loose, billowy trousers gathered into a band at the ankle.

HARRIS TWEED: A trademark for tweed fabrics woven in Scotland.

HEPBURN PANTS: Very tailored ankle length trousers that have fullness all the way to the ankles from a pleated waist.

HERRINGBONE: A pattern produced by intersections of thread or yarn from diagonal lines running across the fabric.

INTARSIA: Bold patterns, usually of flowers, fruit, etc., that are knitted into sweaters.

JACQUARD: A pattern woven into fabrics less textured and lighter in weight than brocade. Designs can be flowers, geometrics, etc.

JERSEY: Very smooth knitted fabric.

LAMBSWOOL: A very fine wool made from the shearlings of lambs.

LUXE: Very rich fabrics such as panne velvet, silk brocade, moiré, satin, cashmere, etc.

MATTE JERSEY: Jersey fabric with a dull matte finish.

MINERAL COLORS: Metallic gold, silver, bronze, pewter, or rust-toned colors.

MONOCHROMATIC: Colors found in a single-hue family. Their only variable is in their intensity and value.

MONOTONE: Simply stated, all one color.

MUFFLER: Long knitted or woven scarf.

MULES: Slippers with high heels, but no ankle straps, that slip or slide on (also referred to as "slides").

NAUTICAL: Clothing based on styling used for Navy or seamen's clothes, usually with navy, red, and/or white motifs.

NEHRU JACKET: Tailored jacket styled on a Mohammedan design, front buttoned, slightly fitted, and usually with a standing collar.

NYLON: Exceptionally strong, nonabsorbent, and durable fiber that has an elastic quality.

OBI: Broad Japanese sash that can be tied several ways.

OPAQUE: A term for a fabric you can't see through.

ORGANZA: Fabric, either of light transparent silk or synthetic silk, having a slight stiffening added for a crisp finish.

PAILLETTES: Large sequins.

PAISLEY PRINT: Colorful design printed on fabric to imitate paisley designs, which, in turn, are repetitive Mideastern designs done in rich appealing color combinations.

PEPLUM: A short flounce around a tightly fitted waistband of a blouse or skirt.

PINWALE CORDUROY: Corduroy having thin ribs or wales with short pile running lengthwise down the fabric.

PLAID: Patterns formed by taking combinations of stripes in varying widths and colors and crossing them at right angles.

POINTELLE: A knitted garment, with a pattern designed on it.

POLO SWEATER OR DRESS: Pullover styled, the sweater or dress is finely knit and short-sleeved, with a collar and front button placket.

PONGEE: A plain weave fabric, silklike and lightweight.

PLAIN WEAVE: A simple weave of crisscross threads.

POORBOY KNIT: T-shirts cut in tank-top styling, made from a thin, ribbed cotton knit, and fit snugly to the body.

POPLIN: A medium weight cotton-type fabric with fine horizontal ribs.

RAGLAN SLEEVES: Sleeves diagonally seamed from neckline to underarm.

SATIN: Fabric with a smooth finish, glossy on one side, matte, or dull on the opposite, made from silk, nylon or rayon.

SEED PEARL: A small, long pearl.

SEERSUCKER: Fabric made from cotton or rayon, and composed of loose yarns alternated with tight warp yarns to create a pucker in the loose yarns.

SHEATH: Straight dress style with no waistline. Waist fitting is accomplished through the use of vertical darts.

SHIRRING: Tight gathering.

RIB WEAVE: A fabric that is woven to have ridges, such as twill or Ottoman.

SILHOUETTE: Contour of a garment seen as a two-dimensional design.

SILK NOIL: Yarn spun from short silk fibers to create a nubby, cottonlike appearance. Used primarily for dresses, blouses, and slacks.

SLUBS: Slightly twisted or thick places in yarn woven into fabric, producing a rough, rustic look.

SPENCER JACKET: A short-waisted jacket, similar to a waiter's.

STIRRUP PANTS: Pants with a belt (of fabric or elastic) running under the heel.

STONEWASHED: Fabric, usually denim, treated to achieve a worn, faded effect. Mostly used on fabric for casual pants, jackets, and skirts.

SYNTHETIC SUEDE: This manmade version of a natural fiber is durable, easy to care for, and is not as expensive as the real thing. Synthetic suede has a few disadvantages: its heavier weight can create a bulky appearance (making the figure look heavier), and it sometimes fades after exposure to sunlight.

TOREADOR PANTS: Tight-fitting pants of a length ranging from just below the knee to just above the ankle.

TRUMPET SKIRT: A slim-fitting skirt with a flare, or trumpet, beginning just above the knee. The fullness of the flare is achieved with inset gores or a bias cut.

TWEED: A rough, twill woolen weave fabric with a fuzzy surface. It can range from a medium to a heavy weight.

UNCONSTRUCTED JACKET: Straight or full jacket, generally unlined, with fewer seams, darts, or shaping.

VISCOSE: Another name for rayon.

VIYELLA: A blend of 55% wool and 45% cotton, generally used for shirts, skirts, dresses, and robes.

VOILE: A sheer, plain weave lightweight fabric, woven closer than gauze, but looser than lightweight cotton.

WORSTED WOOL: A superior process of finishing woolen yarns.

YOKE: Waistband fitted to body contour on pant or skirt. Fitted portion of blouse or dress across shoulders in front or back.

TWILL: A medium weight, ribbed fabric, most usually made from cotton or polyester.

FABRICS AND FABRIC CARE

Natural Fibers	Characteristics	Care
Linen and Cotton	Cool, comfortable to wear, strong, durable, dyes very well, will wrinkle easily unless treated with a wrinkle-resistant finish. Subject to damage by mildew. Burns quickly unless treated with a flame retardant finish.	Bleach only if label indicates it is safe. Remove oily stains before washing, as drying and pressing may set stains permanently. Can be dry-cleaned (check care label).
Mohair	A crisp, resilient slightly scratchy "hand" or feel. Subject to damage by clothes moths and carpet beetles. Burns slowly.	Dry-clean. If wrinkled, press at low heat setting with pressing cloth.
Silk	Strong, luxurious fiber. May tend to water spot. Subject to static electricity. White silk may yellow with age. Low resistance to sun rotting. Subject to damage by carpet beetles.	Dry cleaning is usually preferred. If washable, use moderate temperatures in washing, drying, and pressing. Use a mild soap or detergent. New "washer" silks can be machine washed—read labels carefully and follow the directions.
Wool	Resilient, springs back into shape. Has excellent insulating properties. Subject to damage by clothes moths and carpet beetles. Burns slowly.	Dry cleaning is usually preferred. If washable, use moderate temperatures in washing, drying, and pressing. Use a mild soap.

Man-Made Fibers	Characteristics	Care
Rayon	A cellulose man-made fiber made from a natural substance (wood), it is often considered a natural fiber. It imitates silk, cotton, or wool beautifully, but is less expensive. Rayon lacks elasticity and absorbency and is cool and comfortable.	Rayon shrinks and is usually dry clean only. The new washer rayons are preshrunk. Read label care instructions carefully.
Suede and Leather	Warm, expensive, beautiful, and elegant. Can be also heavy and stiff.	Usually needs expensive professional cleaning by experts.

Miscellaneous Fabric Information

Simple factors affect fabric look, feel, wearability, and durability. You'll be a better shopper and make wiser choices if you understand the characteristics of fabric quality.

Absorbent Fabrics	**Characteristics**
Wool, silk, linen, cotton	Clean easily. Resist wrinkling and static.

Less Absorbent Fabrics	**Characteristics**
Nylon, polyester, rayon	Stain and wrinkle more easily and are prone to static

Blends of fabrics decrease cost, achieve an expensive look at a lower price, make a fabric washable, reduce wrinkling and shrinkage, and increase comfort.

Finishes can change the nature of a fabric. The most widely used finishes can promote easy soil release, a permanent press, water repellency, and sizing/crispness.

Weaves

There are hundreds of weaves and stitches; the five basic varieties of standard weaves are:

1. **Plain**: Each yarn goes under then over
2. **Satin**: Floating yarns pass several crosswise yarns
3. **Dobby or jacquard**: Designs are woven into the fabric
4. **Twill**: A diagonal rib is formed in the weave
5. **Knit**: A series of interlocking loops (such as we make with needles), instead of criss-crossing threads.

Care Tips

The Secrets of Washing Silk

Recently, technical advances have been made in washer silk, which can be washed in the washing machine in warm water. However, silks that are not pre-washed require special care. Here's a simple guide:

1. Do a patch test first to check color fastness. Wet a hidden part of the garment that is not ordinarily visible when you are wearing it (*i.e.*, a bit of the shirt tail of a blouse). Then blot it between two paper towels. If it puckers or loses color, it should be taken to a professional dry cleaner.
2. If the garment is colorfast, wash it gently in cool water with a mild detergent. Silk, like hair, breaks easily and should never be rubbed or wrung.

3. A tablespoonful of white vinegar added to the wash water will help protect against color loss.

4. Rinse out all soap residue in clear cool water. Wrap the garment in a towel to blot excess moisture, then hang on a padded hanger. Dry away from high heat or direct sunlight.

5. Iron the garment inside-out while damp to prevent color change or scorching marks.

6. No time to iron right now? If wrapped in a towel and placed in the freezer, silk later irons beautifully! If the garment is completely dry already, sprinkle it lightly and evenly with water (use a spritzer), wrap in a towel, and place it in the freezer for 15 minutes, then iron.

If your garment label is missing or not clear, the following will prove helpful.

Dry Clean	Machine Wash	Hand Wash
Brocade	Batiste	Antique Fabric
Silk Brocade	Boucle	Antique Lace
Challis	Cambric	Dimity
Crepe (Silk and Jersey)	Chambray	Handkerchief
Foulard	Cotton Knit	Linen
Crepe de Chine	Crepe de Chine (Poly and Cotton)	Viyella (Cold Water)
Gabardine (Silk and Wool)	Denim	Voile (Poly Cotton)
Jacquard	Doeskin	Wool Blends
Knits	Faille	Novelty Knits
Leno	Lame	
Linen	Gingham	
Noil	Jacquard (Poly and Cotton)	
Plissee	Madras	
Rayon	Percale	
Sharkskin	Pique	
Slipper Satin	Polyester	
Taffeta	Pongee	
Velvet	Ramie	
Velveteen	Seersucker	
Viscose	Terry Cloth	
Viyella	Velour	
Voile (Silk)	Washer Silk	
Wool	Washer Rayon	

In the case where the same fabric is listed in more than one care column, you must use your good judgment, and follow the care label.

Stain Removal

All of us have days when our clothes come into contact with accidental spills. Here's an easy step-by-step guide to removing disasters.

Stain	Removal Method
Coffee (Black coffee is easier to remove than creamed coffee.)	Stretch fabric over bowl. Pour equal parts water and vinegar over stain. Then, rinse with water to remove vinegar.
Lipstick	Use K2-R spot remover, spraying a solution of equal parts water and vinegar on any residual stain. Rinse. In an emergency, try using hairspray.
Felt Pen Ink	In a hurry? Use hairspray! Place a paper towel under the stain, wet stain with hairspray. Repeat several times, changing towels.
Mud	Let dry, then brush off. Spray with Shout® or Spray 'n Wash® then wash with detergent and color-safe bleach.
Perspiration	Sponge with a solution made of equal parts water and vinegar. Rinse. Then, soak in a gallon of warm water to which 1 or 2 tablespoons of salt have been added.
Automobile Grease	Use paper towels to remove the excess. Apply Shout® or Spray 'n Wash®. Then apply petroleum jelly to the stain. Wash with detergent and rinse.
Red Wine	Wet stain, apply salt. Let stand 5 minutes. Stretch the fabric over a bowl, then pour boiling water over the stain. Remove any residual stain with a half-water/half-vinegar solution, then rinse.

INDEX